How to Grow

House Plants

By the Editors of Sunset Books
and Sunset Magazine

Lane Publishing Co., Menlo Park, California

Acknowledgments

We wish to extend special thanks, for their helpful advice and assistance, to: Patt and Jack Hudler, Karyn McInnis, Lurlie Moore, and Daphne Smith.

Edited by Kathryn Arthurs

Design: Norman S. Gordon, Roger Flanagan

Illustrations: Dinah James

FRONT COVER: Complementary grouping of house plants enhances the indoor/outdoor feeling of the window wall. Plants are (see diagram at right): (A) *Aglaonema* 'Silver King'; (B) *Chamaedorea elegans;* (C) *Tolmiea menziesii;* (D) *Pilea depressa.* Photographer: Ells Marugg.

BACK COVER: Photographs by Ells Marugg.

Executive Editor, Sunset Books: David E. Clark

Third Printing December 1974

Contents

Using plants indoors

Two-story entry *is perfect showplace for house plant collection. Watering, misting chores can't damage floors.*

Using plants indoors requires more than a good eye for decorating. Indoor gardeners want healthy, thriving house plants to accent various spots around their homes. To be a successful indoor gardener, you'll need to understand the conditions growing plants need to remain healthy: adequate light, correct temperatures, proper humidity level, and the right plant care. Providing these conditions is essential in bringing your house plants to their full potential.

What you need to know about both the esthetics and care of house plants this chapter will tell you. Ideas for various ways of displaying plants — suspending them from walls or ceilings; setting large plants on the floor; placing them on shelves, tables, or plant stands — are also yours for the reading.

HOW PLANTS FUNCTION

Plant survival depends on two interacting processes, photosynthesis and respiration. The products created during one process are utilized in the cycle of the other. A third process, transpiration, causes plants to lose moisture. Understanding these plant processes and what conditions permit them to take place will help you find good indoor locations for growing house plants.

Photosynthesis and respiration

Photosynthesis is the process by which plants manufacture their own food. They take in energy from the sun or light source, carbon dioxide from the air, and water from the soil; these items are combined to create plant sugars. Plant sugars are a versatile food; they can supply energy to the plant immediately, be stored as food for later use, or be used as building material within the plant body. Nutrients taken in from the soil or potting mix help in the production of plant sugars, as well as in the growth of the plant.

While photosynthesis is at work, another process called respiration takes place simultaneously. The plant sugars (created by photosynthesis) are "burned" to create energy for all plant functions. Every portion of a plant — from the topmost leaves to the deepest roots—requires its share of energy to sustain itself. During respiration, oxygen is taken from the air; carbon dioxide is given off as a by-product.

These two processes set up a continuing cycle in which the products of one process are used in the function of the other. This is illustrated at right.

Transpiration

Transpiration is the giving off of a plant's collected moisture through the leaves. Unless this lost moisture is restored, the plant would soon wither and die. Because indoor plants are totally dependent upon their keeper for this needed moisture, good watering practices must be followed to offset transpiration. Watering house plants is discussed in detail on pages 21-24.

One benefit of transpiration is the humidity created when moisture evaporates from leaf surfaces. Grouping house plants together can create a "mini-atmosphere" of humidity (see page 25 for further information).

PROVIDING THE RIGHT CONDITIONS

A good location for growing plants indoors provides the light, temperature, and atmospheric conditions plants need to survive. A house plant placed in a good spot and given the proper care has every opportunity to thrive.

Plants are individual

Each house plant has unique needs as to light, temperature, and humidity. The best way to choose a plant for your house is to first decide on its future location. Study possible indoor locations by asking yourself these questions: Would a house plant enhance this particular spot? How much light is available? What is the average temperature? Are there seasonal changes in light or temperature? How much humidity is present?

Once you answer these questions you will have a profile of your location. The next step is selecting a plant to fill it. Study the Plant Selection Guide, pages 34-95, to find the plant or plants that prefer the environment you have to offer.

If you wish to grow plants unsuited to your location, you can modify the spot to fit a plant's needs. You may provide artificial light, extra humidity (for ways to increase humidity, see pages 24-25), or adjust the room's temperature. Still another solution is to move the plant daily to a location more suited to plant growth and then later return it to the location it decorates. This practice, however, can be time consuming and not too practical.

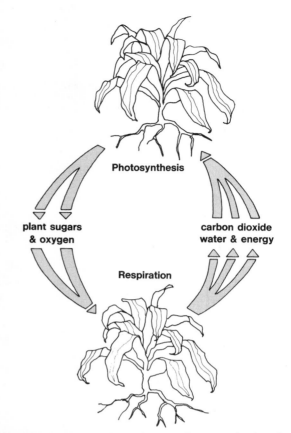

Photosynthesis *cycle shown by top plant; respiration, bottom plant. Arrows indicate interaction.*

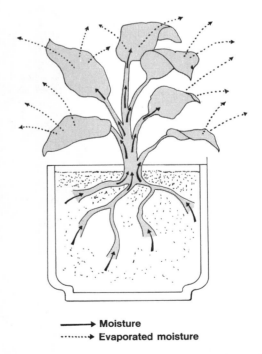

→ Moisture
┄┄┄➤ Evaporated moisture

Arrows *show transpiration cycle; water comes into plant roots, goes through plant, evaporates off leaves.*

Some of us are impulse buyers, choosing a plant for its colorful foliage or interesting flower and giving no thought to its growing needs. If this describes many of your plant purchases, try to find out as much about the plant as possible (either from the Plant Selection Guide, pages 34-95, or from the nurseryman or salesperson where you purchased it). Then find or adapt a location for it. Remember that impulse purchases will probably create more work for you and will not always prove to be successful.

If you begin your house plant shopping with the location firmly in mind and select a plant with the individual needs to fit it, you're on the right track for successful house plant tending.

Light is the limiting factor

Plants need light for photosynthesis (see pages 4-5) but in varying degrees. Blooming plants usually require more light than foliage plants. So do plants that set fruit.

Some plants require direct sunlight; others prefer filtered or low light situations. Another light factor is the amount of time a plant receives light daily. For some plants, shortening days indicate winter and signal the start of their dormancy or rest period.

Plant corner *receives good light from two directions. Bricks on counter surface create buffer zone.*

For others, such as chrysanthemums and Christmas cactus, day length controls their blooming cycle. Day length can be controlled if you wish by adding artificial light or by placing plants in a dark room. To affect the plant's cycle, the addition or deprivation of light must be consistent.

It's best to place plants in a location that provides the light situation they prefer (for light requirements of individual house plants, see the Plant Selection Guide, pages 34-95). But if you decide to place house plants in a location offering less than optimum light, your plant care must change. Since energy and plant building depend upon light, don't expect maximum performance from these plants. Plants grown in limited light should receive less water and fertilizer than the same plants growing in better locations. Repotting should be put off as long as possible. By withholding water and fertilizer and postponing repotting, you will maintain these plants, rather than encouraging them to grow. Maintained plants given limited light, water, and fertilizer should last as long as other house plants; they will remain about the same size and shape indefinitely. The best candidates for maintenance growing situations are those that can tolerate filtered or low light.

Types of available light. The type of light found in indoor situations falls into four main categories:

SUN means direct sunlight coming through a window. An east facing exposure allows morning sun and generally coolish afternoon temperatures. A west window permits afternoon sun with warmer temperatures. A south facing exposure offers sun and warm temperatures most of the day (this is the brightest exposure). Direct sunlight magnified by window glass may raise the temperature to stifling heights that could burn foliage. Most house plants that prefer to bask in sunlight like to be set back from the window pane.

BRIGHT LIGHT can be found in the interior portions of a sunny room or from light reflected from light-colored walls. A plant that prefers this exposure needs it constantly throughout the daylight hours. A north facing exposure provides bright light with no sun.

FILTERED OR DIFFUSED LIGHT is light coming through a lightweight curtain over a window or light that filters into a window through trees or plants growing outdoors. Overhangs or patio roofs also block or filter light.

LOW LIGHT usually refers to dark parts in room interiors, dark corners, or areas without windows. There are few plants that can tolerate these situations; most will need additional light. These areas are prime candidates for artificial lighting.

Using artificial lighting. If the location you choose for growing plants needs supplemental lighting to be effective, providing artificial lighting may be the answer. Plants can also benefit from a combination of natural and artificial light during the short, gray days of winter.

Special fluorescent tubes have been developed to simulate actual sunlight rays and are used to stimulate plants to bloom, produce fruit, and set seeds. These are slightly more expensive than regular fluorescent tubes and are readily available.

Plain fluorescent lights can supply sufficient light for plant growth. They can also be used in combination with the less expensive incandescent bulbs. Incandescent lights should not be used alone; they are not strong enough in the red and blue color bands that plants need and they generate too much heat for sensitive plants.

Whether you buy a lighting unit or make one, provide some method of adjusting the height to allow for plant growth and different-sized containers. Start with the tubes 6 to 12 inches above the foliage. If the foliage bunches together unnaturally, plants are receiving too much light. If they become leggy, provide more light. Fluorescent lighting will not harm plants, so the light may be set as close as needed.

Fixtures need a white or foil reflector to direct light onto plants. When placing plants under it, remember the light at the center of the tube is the strongest. Several fluorescent tubes placed side by side are best; one tube alone will not support plant life that depends solely on this light. A standard amount of light for all plants is 15 to 20 watts of light for every square foot of growing surface.

Most plants require a period of darkness every 24 hours (even plants need their sleep). Most foliage plants need 10 to 12 hours of light a day; flowering plants require 16. A regular schedule is important to healthy plant growth. An inexpensive timer can be used to regulate the lights.

Some like it hot

And some plants like cold temperatures. Luckily, the majority of house plants adjust readily to normal indoor temperatures. Since people as well as plants occupy rooms, it's best to select plants that prefer the same temperature levels you do. Unless you wish to provide a special plant room or a greenhouse that caters to specific temperature needs, leave finicky plants to more advanced gardeners.

Temperature levels found in most home situations fall into three main categories: cool (55°-65°), average (65°-75°), and warm (75°-85°).

Avoid exposing plants to drastic temperature changes and drafts. Windows may be many degrees hotter or colder than the room interior. Check the temperature near windows where plants are kept during extreme weather conditions (either hot or cold conditions, since both extremes can be devastating), and move plants if necessary. Other locations

White walls *reflect enough light for Boston fern. Metal plant stand permits air circulation.*

Book case *provides limited light. Use plants tolerant of low light situations.*

Table-top unit *adjusts to various heights, provides artificial light for group of house plants.*

Trailing plant *cascades down book case; unit serves as room divider for living room, dining room.*

to avoid are on or near heat registers, radiators, or fireplaces, or in the direct blast of air conditioning.

Humidity levels are closely related to house temperatures: the warmer the air, the faster humidity in the air is dispelled. (Warm temperatures also speed up transpiration in plants, see page 5.) This is especially true when a home's central heating unit is in use, creating a hot dry atmosphere. Many plants we grow indoors need humidity to survive and depend upon us to provide it. Ways to increase humidity levels indoors are discussed on pages 24-25.

DECORATING WITH HOUSE PLANTS

Whether you use plants strictly as decorative accents (and replace them when they begin to look forlorn) or find caring for plants as enjoyable as having them grace your home, your approach to growing and displaying plants indoors will be as unique and individual as your own personality. Your use of house plants is limited only by the space you have available and your imagination.

As with everything else, conventional plant placements are rapidly being replaced by innovative displays. Plant containers (discussed on pages 10-13) and the necessity of watering (see pages 21-24 for further information) will also need to be considered both for appearance and convenience.

The following section describes some of the ways house plants can be displayed. Use the suggestions or adapt them to your particular situation.

House tree *graces corner of dining room. White walls provide reflected light, are good background.*

Marble-topped table *in entry displays large vining plant in copper pot. Lamp supplies extra light.*

The house tree. Large, treelike plants make a strong statement in your house. Planted in capacious containers, they can accent an entry or a view, fill an empty corner, hide a problem area, or divide indoor spaces into smaller, more usable areas.

Care can present a problem. Sheer size necessitates keeping large plants stationary; watering, fertilizing, and maintenance will take place on the spot. Another problem is to protect your floor surfaces or carpets from water damage—a "buffer zone" (see page 14) is a good solution.

Hanging plants. Any house plant with a drooping or spreading growth habit can be hung to advantage. Possible locations are in windows, corners of rooms, or around skylights. Just hang them out of the way of foot traffic—bumping into a heavy hanging plant isn't healthy for the person or the plant.

How to suspend the plant and how to water it once it's up are two major problems. A well-watered house plant and its container can weigh up to 50 pounds. It's best to place the hook or bracket that holds the plant into a wall stud or ceiling joist for maximum support. If the best location is nowhere near a stud or joist and you must rely on gypsum wall board to hold the plant, use a toggle bolt or a spreading fastener; these help provide better weight distribution.

Whenever possible, use plastic plant containers for your hanging plants—they weigh much less than clay or ceramic pots, they won't absorb any moisture, and plants in them require less water.

Watering is still another dilemma. A watered plant will drip. To prevent this, either provide a drip saucer (see pages 13-14) to catch excess water (a commercial tray that clips onto the bottom of hanging plants is available) or take the plant down to water it and let it drain completely before rehanging.

Put your plants on a pedestal. Plants set on a plant stand become a living piece of sculpture. Whether the pedestal is metal and glass, intricately turned wrought iron, a small wooden table, a turned wooden post, or a marble column, both the stand and the plant will receive compliments. It's best to use plants on plant stands in an empty corner, a window, or on a fairly blank wall so nothing distracts from their beauty.

Care presents few problems. Drip saucers and the plant stand surface protect furniture, floors, and carpets from water damage. Be sure your stand is stable; a top-heavy plant could cause a precariously balanced stand to topple.

Placing plants around the room. Whether you use plants on tables, book shelves, mantles, or other interior surfaces, the plants and their containers form a decorative accent. Choose healthy plants that are sized proportionally for the space they will occupy. Attractive foliage or colorful flowers are always a bonus.

The container can add almost as much as the plant to the overall decorative effect. Choosing the proper container is discussed on pages 10-14. Decorative sleeve containers (see page 14) offer one solution to the drip problem and make it easier to move plants from place to place. A "buffer zone" (see page 14) may be necessary to protect furniture surfaces.

BUYERS' GUIDE TO HEALTHY PLANTS

When purchasing a house plant, you need to consider two things: the plant you select and where you purchase it. Be choosy; don't settle for the first plant you see.

As with any service or product you pay for, find a reputable house plant dealer. You may have good luck with bargain plants, but it's best to buy from a nursery, plant boutique, or florist shop where plants are given proper treatment.

If you are a wise shopper, the house plant you select will meet these criteria:

1. Survey the general plant selection. Do most plants seem healthy and happy? Overall excellence of products usually signifies good merchandise and proper care of house plants.

2. Look at the plant itself. Does it look healthy: Is it free from leaf damage and pests? Is the color good? Does it have a pleasing shape? Is the leaf size consistent? Does it show any new growth? If the answer to all these questions is "Yes," your choice is probably a good one.

3. Check to see if the plant is potbound. If any plant roots are peeking through the drainage hole, the plant has been in that pot too long. It's best to make another selection.

4. Choose a plant the size you want it. If you want a large house plant, don't buy a small version and wait for it to grow. It could take months or years. A larger plant that is better established should adapt to a new environment more readily.

Planting in containers

Pebbles *add finishing touch to decorative sleeve planting by hiding dirt, clay pot rim, rock filler.*

You've found the perfect house plant and selected its new location. The next step? Select a container and a potting mix—then put them all together.

A plant container does more than hold the potting mix and house plant: it also provides decoration. Plants used indoors become room accessories, and their containers help considerably in making them effective. Choose containers that will suit the plants and enhance their location.

This chapter provides you with information on available plant containers, potting mixes, and planting techniques. Planting in drainless and self-watering containers and using decorative sleeve containers are also covered.

CHOOSING A CONTAINER

When selecting a plant container, the indoor gardener need no longer settle for the ubiquitous red clay pot. A myriad of choices is possible.

With the rebirth of house plant popularity, manufacturers have responded by offering a wide variety of containers in many sizes, shapes, colors, and materials. Indoor gardeners can also utilize decorative sleeves—large containers of metal, wicker, or ceramic too special for direct planting—to hold potted plants for display purposes.

Your main consideration in choosing a container is your plant's growing needs. The size of the container will be determined by the plant's size. Put your plant in a pot that's the same size as its present container or in one that is ½ to 1 inch larger in diameter. Avoid potting a plant in too small or too large a container.

Different types of containers offer growing advantages for plants with special needs. Plastic pots and other non-porous containers keep soil damp the longest—a good situation for moisture-loving plants. Porous pots, such as red clay, allow air circulation around root systems; this hastens moisture loss in potting mix, good for plants that prefer a dry out between waterings. Study your house plant's growth requirements very carefully and then consult the

Plant Selection Guide on pages 34-95 before purchasing its container.

Look for house plant containers in nurseries, indoor plant stores, garden supply stores, antique stores, craft shops or craft fairs, hardware stores, stores that specialize in home accessories, or any other store that might sell garden or house plant supplies.

Types of containers

Before purchasing your house plant's container, familiarize yourself with the possibilities. You'll find almost as many different kinds of containers available as house plants.

Some general points to keep in mind: 1) Try to find containers with drainage holes. You can plant in a drainless container, but plant care is much more difficult (see pages 17-18 for instructions). 2) Choose the container that best meets your plant's growth needs. 3) Select a container that will accent your interior decoration. Plants and their containers become an integral part of each room they are placed in and should be used advantageously. 4) Try to purchase a drip saucer (see pages 13-14) at the same time you buy the container. Size and compatibility are easier to judge with the container in hand.

Clay pots. That old standby, the red clay pot, continues to be popular. It's inexpensive, easy to find, and available in many shapes and sizes. The earthy color (besides red, clay pots are sometimes available in shades of brown or gray) and texture blend well with most furniture styles, and the pot doesn't overshadow the plant.

Clay pots are porous, allowing them to absorb moisture and permit air circulation. Clay pots are great for beginning gardeners because it's difficult (but not impossible) to overwater plants in them.

If plants are overfertilized, excess salts appear as a white crust on the pot sides. In areas where the water has a heavy salt concentration, the excess salts leach out, also forming a white crust on pot sides. A non-porous container cannot give you these problem signals.

Plastic pots. Modern man's answer to pottery is plastic. Plastic containers are easy to clean, light-weight even when watered, inexpensive to buy, and available in a wide variety of colors, shapes, and sizes. One novel container is made of clear plastic, exposing the potting mix and root system.

Non-porous plastic pots may create watering problems. They do not absorb any moisture or permit air circulation. Since watered plants in plastic pots remain moist longer than plants in porous containers and need watering less frequently, it's best to use plastic pots for moisture-loving plants. But the beginning indoor gardener may find porous pots

Pewter pitcher *holds fleshy-leafed succulent. Keep plant in original pot inside pitcher for good drainage.*

easier to use until watering plants has become second nature.

If wide slits on the container bottom serve as drainage holes, use a thin layer of stones or pebbles instead of pot shards for crocking.

Glazed ceramic pots. Available in many colors and sometimes vividly decorated with patterns or pictures, glazed ceramic pots are quite ornamental. Prices vary according to size and decoration.

Glazed containers, like plastic pots, are non-porous and may present watering problems to the beginner. If you find the perfect glazed pot but are hesitant to buy it because of possible watering difficulties, use it as a decorative sleeve (see page 14 for directions).

Metal containers. With the renewed interest in indoor gardening, an increasing number of people use house plants as decorative objects. Plants in metal containers of copper, brass, silver or silverplate, pewter, polished steel, iron, or aluminum are impressive and elegant enough to suit any decor.

For various reasons, most metal containers are best used as decorative sleeves (see page 14). Since many metals tarnish, they may require periodic cleaning or polishing. If excess water is left standing indefinitely in the pot, it could corrode the metals. If your container is valuable, line the inside with heavy plastic or place a drainage saucer inside to avoid water damage.

Metal containers rarely have drainage holes. If you decide to plant directly into your metal pot, drainage material (see pages 17-18) must be provided to capture any excess moisture created by regular waterings. If you are lucky enough to find a metal pot with proper drainage holes, treat it as a normal container when planting. Be sure to provide a saucer or tray to catch any water runoff.

Plant roots that touch the sides or bottom of a copper pot will die. This shouldn't radically affect the plant's health, however, since the remaining roots will continue to survive.

Wooden containers. Though more generally used outdoors, wooden containers are relatively inexpensive and available in many sizes, shapes, and wood types.

Stained or varnished wood is usually non-porous. Untreated wood containers can be porous and should be soaked before you plant in them. If drainage holes are present, place a waterproof saucer under the pot to catch excess water.

If your wooden container is slatted, the sides may not be watertight. This could create a seepage problem that would be unattractive, as well as hard on furniture surfaces. It's best to use these containers as decorative sleeves (see page 14) rather than planting in them directly.

Baskets. Plants and basketry seem to be made for each other. Baskets can be found in a profusion of shapes, sizes, and price ranges. Although usually constructed of natural materials in shades of beige or brown, some woven containers are painted or stained in a variety of colors.

Since baskets aren't watertight, it's best to use them as decorative sleeves (see page 14). Unless a saucer to catch water runoff can be placed inside the basket, watered plants will leak, probably ruining both furniture surfaces and eventually the basket. Baskets can be waterproofed to prevent water damage (see page 19).

A few baskets can be purchased with metal inserts, permitting planting in them directly. Since these inserts do not have drainage holes, treat them as drainless containers when planting.

Self-watering containers. If you find watering house plants a nuisance or if you travel frequently and

Plant containers: *Vive la différence!*

must leave your plants alone, self-watering containers may be the answer. These innovative, recently introduced containers are usually constructed of plastic. They have a reservoir for storing water and a method of tapping this stored water when the potting soil dries out. Moving through capillary action, water is drawn up into the pot by either a sensing device or a fiber wick until the potting mix becomes evenly moist. When potting mix dries out again, the cycle is repeated.

Use the self-watering container as a decorative sleeve (see page 14) or plant directly into it.

Eclectic containers. If your taste leans to the unusual or the unexpected, you can put plants in containers originally designed for another purpose. Cookie jars, ice buckets, pitchers, coffee pots, jars, watering cans, or anything else with enough space to hold potting mix and a plant can be transformed into unique containers. You only need imagination and courage.

Since these containers were not designed to hold plants, they will not have drainage holes. Follow the planting instructions for drainless containers on pages 17-18 or use them as decorative sleeves (see page 14).

Catch that drip!

If you correctly water a house plant growing in a container that has proper drainage, you're going to have a drip problem. Any excess water that the potting mix can't retain during the normal watering will run out the drainage holes. Wherever you display house plants, this runoff will probably be troublesome. The most efficient solution is to provide a saucer to catch the excess water.

Many containers are sold with matching saucers. Whenever possible, buy a drip saucer or tray at the same time you purchase a container. With other plant containers, it's up to the indoor gardener to find a suitable drip saucer. Look for unobtrusive saucers or trays. Although a mismatched saucer may protect furniture surfaces, it can ruin the visual effect of the house plant. Pads or mats may also be used to protect interior surfaces.

Part of the runoff problem can be solved at watering time. Take house plants to a sink for watering;

Cork coaster *keeps ceramic container off of wooden table surface, helps prevent water damage.*

Wooden blocks *cut to fit create buffer zone between clay pot, tiled floor.*

Wrought iron ring *made to support clay saucer creates air space between drainage saucer and carpet.*

then let them drain in the sink for a while (at least 10 minutes). The majority of excess water should drain into the sink, not into the drip saucer. (This method of watering does not eliminate the need for a drip saucer.)

If your drip saucer or tray is made of a porous material, such as red clay, it can absorb moisture. You can paint the interior of a clay saucer with silicone paint to waterproof it; this eliminates the absorption problem. Water sitting in non-porous saucers, such as plastic or glazed ceramic, may cause condensation on the saucer's exterior. If the saucers with absorbed moisture or condensation remain in one spot long enough, the contact may eventually ruin furniture surfaces or rot carpets.

Many indoor gardeners protect interior surfaces by creating a "buffer zone" between drip saucers and furniture, floors, or carpets. This buffer zone forms an air pocket in which any absorbed moisture or moisture caused by condensation can be dissipated. Coasters, mats, blocks of wood, metal or wooden plant holders, or any other means of raising the plant container and saucer off furniture or carpet surfaces creates a buffer zone. This created air pocket helps eliminate the chance of any water damage. Several types of buffer zones are pictured at the left.

Using decorative sleeves

A decorative sleeve is any container that already-potted house plants are set into for display purposes. The decorative sleeve has many advantages: 1) Valuable or easily damaged containers are protected from any damage direct planting may have caused. 2) A sick plant can be replaced quickly with a healthy plant, avoiding the need to transplant which is time-consuming for you and hard on an ailing plant. 3) Many decorative sleeves are watertight, eliminating the need for a drip saucer or tray. 4) If you display plants in a poor growing location, such as a dark hall, you can rotate several plants between a good growing location and the location of a decorative sleeve placed in a spot with bad lighting. This keeps your plants in a healthy condition.

Utilizing decorative sleeves is easy. The sleeve should always be at least one inch larger in diameter than the plant's container to allow for good air circulation. Put the potted house plant into the sleeve. If it sits too low in the sleeve, prop it up. Bricks, other clay pots turned upside down, layers of small rocks or pebbles, sphagnum moss, or any material that will raise the potted plant to the proper level can be used. This also allows for drainage, keeping plants in decorative sleeves from sitting in water. Some examples of utilizing decorative sleeves are on the next page.

Decorative sleeves: *Ceramic, copper, or wicker can show off your plants*

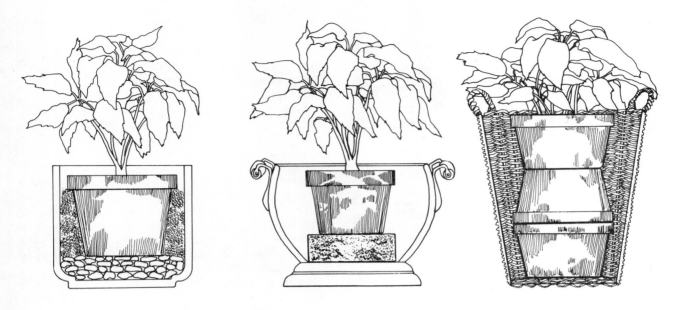

Decorative sleeves *display potted plants. From left: layer of pebbles supports potted plant inside the ceramic sleeve; copper bucket contains plant raised by brick; clay pots lift plant to top of wicker basket.*

If the runoff from normal watering could damage your decorative sleeve, line it with heavy plastic or provide a drip saucer inside the sleeve under the potted plant as a preventive measure.

Some indoor gardeners also line the space between the plant container and the sleeve to give the illusion of direct planting. Sphagnum moss or pebbles are commonly used; loosely packed, they still permit adequate air circulation around the container. A top mulch of pebbles or bark covering both the soil surface of the plant and the liner help add to this illusion (see the photograph on page 10).

THE PLANTING MEDIUM

Potting mix is the all-important ingredient for healthy plants. It forms the medium in which plants live and grow; it provides the initial nutrients plants need; and it permits moisture retention while allowing any excess water to drain away.

Commercial potting mixes

For most indoor gardeners, buying a package of prepared potting mix is the most efficient method of selecting house plant soil. Potting mix is sold in varying sized packages, so you can purchase only the amount you need at the time. (Reseal any left-over potting mix in the package for use later.)

Use a commercial mix specifically formulated for house plants. It provides the nutrients that plants will initially need; you can replenish these nutrients when necessary with a house plant fertilizer (see page 25). The packaged potting mix has been sterilized to eliminate any pests or diseases that might be present. These mixes are readily available at nurseries, indoor plant stores, or other stores where garden supplies are sold.

Some light-weight mixes may need to be moistened before planting. Squeeze a handful of soil in your fist; the mix should be damp enough to form a compact ball when you release it yet will not be dripping wet. If the mix is dry and crumbly, add enough water to the mix to make it cohesive.

If you want to make your own

If purchasing a commercial potting mix in a plastic bag isn't your idea of returning to the soil indoors, you can make your own. Blend equal amounts of coarse sand (be sure the sand you add has been washed; the salt in unwashed sea sand may damage tender plants), garden loam or good garden topsoil, and peat moss or fir bark. To each two quarts of this mix, add ½ cup each charcoal and perlite.

Every ingredient in your potting mix has a purpose. Garden loam or topsoil contains particles of clay that hold fertilizing materials in an available state for plant roots. Sand, perlite, and leaf mold hold air around the roots, which is essential to good

Baking soil smells unpleasant, but the heat destroys any pests, weed seeds, or plant diseases present.

Container preparation

Always plant in a clean container. Wash containers in soap and water; rinse them well to remove any soap film.

Resurrected containers, especially red clay pots, may require scrubbing with a wire or a stiff-bristled brush to remove any clinging soil or salt and algae buildup.

Soak all porous containers, such as red clay pots, in water prior to planting. Dry, porous containers may rob moisture from the potting mix and the newly transplanted plant. Immerse the pots in water for an hour or so; then let them dry for a short time.

Never put a plant in too large a container; you'll have too much soil for too few roots. The roots can't extract water from the extra soil, and the surplus moisture may eventually rot the roots. Choose a container the same size as the one holding your house plant or one only slightly larger—a pot ½ to 1 inch larger in diameter is the maximum. If your present container is larger than 10 inches in diameter, you may wish to use a somewhat larger pot to avoid frequent transplanting.

Planting—step-by-step

Transplanting is a messy business, so work in an easy-to-clean area. Work quickly to avoid transplanting shock to the plant. If you are interrupted, cover the exposed root ball with damp towels, either paper or cloth, and return to the transplanting as soon as possible.

Gather together the house plant, the potting mix, the cleaned container, and any other needed materials and begin the transplanting:

1) Remove the plant from its present container, keeping the root ball intact. Knock it out according to the instructions on page 28.

Plants in metal nursery containers can be cut out. Slit the sides of the container, pull them away from the plant, and remove the root ball. Use tin snips or a can cutter or ask the nurseryman to do it for you.

2) Place pot shards (curved, broken bits of old clay pots) or pebbles over the drain hole. If you use pebbles, be sure they can't plug the drainage hole. This prevents the potting mix from draining out of the pot every time the plant is watered. If you use pot shards, place them over the drainage hole so the curved surface faces downward, as shown in the illustration.

3) Put enough potting mix in the pot to bring the surface of the root ball about ½ inch from the container rim. (You may want to leave more space in larger pots to keep things in proportion.) This level seems to work best for watering plants. See illustration 3.

4) Center the root ball in the container and fill in the sides with potting mix. Occasionally, thump the

plant growth. Leaf mold also provides some nutrients. Charcoal bits keep the soil "sweet." These ingredients are usually available at most nurseries, garden supply stores, or indoor plant stores.

Any potting mix that you make yourself which contains garden soil must be sterilized. Garden loam or topsoil may contain pests, weed seeds, or plant diseases; sterilizing the mix eliminates these problems. Follow these steps to sterilize your soil: 1) Mix all ingredients thoroughly. 2) Dampen the mix slightly with water; then spread it in shallow oven-proof pans. Be sure the mix is no more than 4 inches deep. 3) Place the filled pans in a 180° oven and bake for at least two hours (see the photograph, at top). An alternate method is to cover the soil-filled pans with kitchen foil or clear baking wrap and seal. Insert a cooking thermometer through the center of the covering into the soil but not touching the pan. Place in the oven and heat until the soil temperature reaches 180°; keep the temperature at that level—no higher—for 30 minutes.

Prepare yourself for the nasty odor of baking soil. Luckily this odor isn't lasting. Remove the sterilized soil from the oven and let it air for a few days. Store it in sturdy paper or plastic bags.

POTTING PLANTS

Potting brings it all together: your house plant, its new container, and the potting mix in which it will live. Before you begin to repot, have all the necessary materials ready and waiting. Finding yourself out of potting mix with the new container half filled can be frustrating.

container on your working surface to settle in the new soil (see illustrations 4 and 5).

Continue to add potting mix until the sides are level with the root ball surface. Be careful not to bury the root ball. Plants can suffocate, too.

5) Smooth out the surface of the new potting mix with your fingers. Don't push down on the root ball or the plant stem; this could damage fragile hair roots.

6) Water your newly potted plant thoroughly; then step back and admire. Once your plant adjusts to its new container, you can move it to its permanent location.

Planting in a drainless container

Putting a house plant in a container without a drainage hole isn't ideal, but it can be done. Problems arise when the plant is watered; once in, the water has no escape. The solution is to provide a drainage layer inside the container. This layer acts as a holding tank for the excess moisture.

Place a layer of small rocks or pebbles in the bottom of the container. This layer should take up about one quarter of the total container volume. (You can also use small pieces of lava or "feather rock" or broken bits of clay pots for the drainage

Transplanting: *Step-by-step directions*

1. Remove plant *and root ball intact from original container.*

2. Cover drainage hole *with pebbles or pot shards; add some potting mix.*

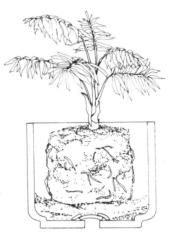

3. Fill container *with soil until root ball surface is near pot rim.*

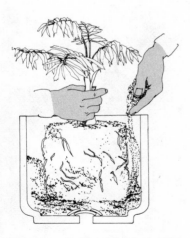

4. Center root ball *and begin to fill in sides with potting mix.*

5. Thump pot *carefully on working surface to settle potting mix.*

6. Smooth soil surface *gently with fingers; avoid plant stem area.*

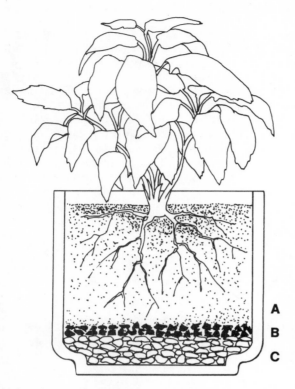

Soil layers *inside a drainless container are shown: (A) potting mix, (B) charcoal, (C) drainage material.*

material.) This drainage layer allows water to seep through the soil and retains it until the moisture can be utilized by the plant or evaporated. It also keeps the plant roots from sitting in soggy soil and permits the roots to obtain oxygen.

Spread a thin layer of charcoal bits directly over the drainage layer. Charcoal keeps the soil "sweet" by absorbing any noxious by-products created in decaying matter in the soil or potting mix.

Begin putting in the potting mix and proceed with the transplanting as described on page 16. The various layers used in a drainless container are illustrated at left.

The adjustment period

A newly potted plant needs a respite from its normal environment. Adjusting to a new container can be traumatic for a plant.

Place the well-watered plant in a cool, sunless spot for several days. If it wilts, don't rewater unless the potting mix is completely bone dry to the touch. Try misting to rejuvenate the plant. Or create a greenhouse atmosphere by sealing the plant, pot and all, in a plastic bag. (A sun-loving plant is an exception; place it immediately in its permanent location.)

Once it has adjusted to potting, move your plant to its permanent location.

Basket *will serve as decorative sleeve container for bird's nest fern; larger size permits air circulation.*

Newly planted garden *in old watering can gets its first watering; plants will need time to adjust to new situation.*

HOW TO MAKE BASKETS HOLD WATER

Though woven baskets make good house plant containers, watering the plants presents the problem of leakage. Lining the basket with a plastic bag or aluminum foil is a possible solution, but inevitably the plastic tears or the foil breaks. The best answer is to coat the basket interior with polyester resin and strips of newspaper to make it waterproof and rot-resistant.

You'll need clear polyester resin and hardener (they come in separate containers), a brush, acetone to clean the brush, and some newspaper strips. A quart of resin is enough for about three baskets of wastepaper basket size.

Cut the newspaper into 4-inch-wide strips the length of the basket bottom diameter plus about 10 inches (allow the strips to go up about 5 inches on each side). Make sure you work outdoors or in a very well-ventilated area; the resin fumes are both dangerous and strong-smelling. Protect your hands with gloves.

To prepare one basket, thoroughly mix about a third of the resin with a proportionate amount of hardener according to the directions on the can (if you're doing a very large basket, mix more of the resin). Brush the mixture on the basket bottom and up the sides about 5 inches. Place a strip of newspaper to cover this. Continue with the alternate pattern of resin and paper strips (crisscrossing the strips to cover the bottom) until you

have about eight coats of paper. Pour any remaining resin mixture into the bottom of the basket and let it harden. Check to be sure you have a complete seal. If there's any leakage when you pour in water, let the basket dry and then mix up some more resin and recoat the paper-covered area.

Once the basket has been waterproofed, it's ready for a house plant. You may plant directly into the basket following directions for planting in a drainless container (see pages 17-18 for information) or use the basket as a decorative sleeve container. Place plants planted in clay pots or other containers into the basket. A layer of rocks or a drip saucer will keep the pot from sitting directly in water.

Climbing philodendron *is growing inside a clay pot. When watered, it drains into water-tight basket.*

Line basket *with alternating layers of 4-inch-wide newspaper strips and resin-hardener mixture.*

Caring for your house plants

Plant care *is an individual matter. Each plant has different watering, light, and fertilizing needs.*

Like any working unit—either living or mechanical—a plant needs proper maintenance to function normally. A plant grown indoors in a pot is completely dependent upon its caretaker for light, water, and nutrients. It requires the right amount of water, pruning to stay a reasonable size, repotting when its container becomes restrictive, and protection when diseases or pests attack.

This chapter gives you the instructions needed to maintain healthy house plants. Inspecting plants for possible problems and the need for humidity, watering, fertilizing, pruning, and repotting techniques are explained in detail. Consistent and careful attention to your plants' needs will allow them to function properly in their indoor environment.

ROUTINE INSPECTION

Inspecting house plants on a day-to-day basis or at regular intervals is a habit worth developing. Just a few minutes a day will help keep your plants in peak condition. This careful attention also enables you to correct most problems before they become major.

Ask yourself several questions during the routine check: 1) Does the plant need watering? 2) Has dust accumulated on the leaves? 3) Are any brown or dying leaves visible? 4) Is there any sign of a pest infestation? If the answer to any of these questions is "Yes," see the appropriate section below for a possible solution.

Watering frequency. Plants require varying amounts of water. Some like to be constantly moist, whereas others prefer to dry out between waterings. Know your plant's water preference; the Plant Section Guide on pages 34-95 includes the necessary watering information for most common house plants.

There are several methods of checking the amount of moisture present in the potting mix. Experiment until you find the best method for you. Methods of checking moisture levels in potted plants are discussed on page 22-23.

Dust accumulation. Plants—like furniture—benefit from regular dusting. Wash dirty leaves individually with plain water on a soft cloth or cotton. Always support a leaf with one hand and gently wipe off dust with the other.

Some plant keepers recommend occasional showers for their plants; use a spray attachment in a sink, a hose with a sprayer in the yard, or a bathroom shower. If you have a water softener, spray the plant outdoors with a hose. Water from outdoor faucets usually bypasses the water softener. Be sure to let plants drip dry before returning them to their normal places. Remember to limit outdoor excursions for tender house plants to the warmer seasons of the year.

Daily misting (see page 24) also helps keep dust from building up on plant foliage.

Brown or dying leaves. Keep your house plants looking fresh and healthy by removing any unsightly leaves. The dead or dying leaves ruin the plant's appearance and may invite unwanted pests or disease. Removing dead leaves or branches also makes room for new growth; use scissors or a sharp knife.

Many leaves develop brown tips or edges, usually caused by a lack of humidity. Some indoor gardeners recommend trimming these unsightly edges off to keep up appearances. Use sharp scissors to cut off brown tips or edges; try to follow the natural leaf shape so the trim isn't obvious. Of course, this trimming won't correct the problem; it merely improves the plant's looks. Try to correct the situation as soon as possible. Causes of brown leaf tips and edges are discussed on page 31.

Pests. Most pests that attack house plants are small and hard to see. Your first indication of a problem will probably be poor plant health, which shows up as yellow or dying foliage, stunted growth, or curled or distorted foliage. Examine sickly plants closely. If pests seem to be the problem, refer to the section on pests and their control (see pages 31-33) for a solution. If you find no sign of small creatures on your sickly plant, make sure your plant is receiving the care and culture it requires. To familiarize yourself with your plant's requirements, see the Plant Selection Guide on pages 34-95.

HOW TO WATER WISELY

Watering is perhaps the most important service you can give your house plants. More plants fail from improper watering than from any other cause. The best way to avoid overwatering — the most common watering offense — is to familiarize yourself with each plant's watering needs.

Watering is usually done in the morning. Many gardeners fill their watering cans the night before to allow the water to reach room temperature. This also permits any chlorine to evaporate.

Watering hanging plants *is easy with long spout. Containers have drainage saucer to eliminate drips.*

If your water is softened in a water softener or if it's remarkably hard or tastes of salts or minerals, use bottled or distilled water. If your outdoor water faucets bypass the water softener, draw your water there. Be sure to let the water reach room temperature before using it on plants. Some plant lovers catch rainwater in a cistern and water their plants with it.

"How much water?" is the initial question most people ask when acquiring a plant. Most indoor plant specialists will respond evasively. Typical answers are, "As much as it needs"; "Not too much, yet not too little"; and the all-time favorite — "It depends." For watering is a very individual matter. How much and how often you water a plant depend on the nature of the plant and the environment it grows in. Water when your plant needs it, not according to a schedule that's convenient for you.

Factors that affect watering

Since no two plants have the same water requirement, many factors beyond the control of you or your plant will affect the amount of water it needs. Yet some of these factors, such as the type of container you select, you *can* control and use to your plant's advantage.

The seasons. In winter, when days are short and skies often gray, house plants generally need less water than during the summertime. Some plants

Washing plants *off is easy in a sink with sprayer hose attachment. Force of water removes dust, any pests.*

Remove leaves *that are damaged or dead carefully with scissors. Use scissors to trim brown tips, edges.*

respond to winter by retreating into a state of listlessness. They don't require much water; instead, give them dry aid and comfort by continuing your routine inspections and making sure they have adequate light. When your listless plant perks up, resume its normal care.

Plant dormancy. Some plants have a season for going completely dormant. Dormancy is a period of inactivity or non-growth. The foliage of most tuberous and bulbous plants (the plants most likely to have dormant periods) begins to yellow after the plants bloom. Gradually withhold water from these plants until the top foliage is dry. Then store the pots with the tubers or bulbs in a cool, dry, out-of-the-way spot. When new growth appears, restore the plant to its customary place.

Containers. The container you choose to hold your plant will affect the amount of water needed and how often you apply it. (Plant containers are discussed in more detail on pages 10-13.)

RED CLAY POTS are porous, absorbing moisture and permitting good air circulation. Plants growing in clay pots tend to use more water and need it more frequently than plants in other types of containers. Moisture levels of plants in clay pots will need to be checked frequently.

PLASTIC POTS are non-porous; potting mix in them tends to retain moisture for longer periods of time than mix in clay pots. Overwatering can be a real problem. Most gardeners reserve plastic pots for their moisture-loving plants.

GLAZED POTS, usually made of clay that is painted with a ceramic glaze, are also non-porous. Treat plants in glazed pots like those in plastic pots.

POTS WITHOUT DRAINAGE present a problem. Once a plant is watered in an undrained pot, moisture remains in the potting mix until it is utilized or evaporated. Plants in drainless pots should receive less water than those in containers with drain holes. Just water a portion of the soil surface of these plants. A good rule-of-thumb is to add water equal to one-fourth of the total volume of the container. Watch these plants carefully for signs of improper watering.

One method of watering plants in pots without drainage is to insert a funnel into the soil with the funnel tip an inch under the soil surface (see photo on next page). Pour water into the mouth of the funnel until water no longer goes through it.

Plant differences. Plants that grow quickly and those that bloom or bear fruit heavily need more water than plants with a more conservative life style. Plants with a large total leaf surface, such as ferns, require more water than sparsely foliaged plants. Plants with soft, lush foliage need more water than those with waxy, leathery, or succulent leaves.

Does your plant need water?

Indoor gardeners use many different methods for judging when a plant needs to be watered. Experiment with various methods of testing moisture levels and then adapt the one you find most effective.

The touch test. Most indoor gardeners agree that this is the best method to judge a plant's need for water. Feel the soil surface with your finger. If the potting mix is dry to a depth of ½ to 1 inch, add water. If the potting mix is still moist, keep checking the plant periodically, as often as daily.

Drooping foliage. Drooping or wilted foliage on a house plant usually indicates it needs water fast! Water a wilted plant thoroughly; then wait. After several hours the plant should resume its normal appearance. House plants usually survive this wilting once or twice, but not indefinitely. Constantly wilting plants indicate poor gardening habits. For your plant's sake, don't rely on this method for judging water needs.

The weight test. Some people judge a potted plant's water needs by the weight of the pot. This is the rule-of-thumb: the lighter the pot, the less moisture present in the potting mix. To effectively judge the moisture present using this method, you must know what the pot and plant weigh both when well watered and when in need of water. This method is best left to the experienced gardener.

Tink . . . tunk! Some gardeners claim they can tell when a potted plant needs water by tapping the pot. If it sounds like "tink," it doesn't require water; if it goes "tunk," it needs water. To use this method, a good ear for "tinks" and "tunks" is necessary. The people who have it are probably the same ones who can tell a ripe watermelon by thumping it. This method also works best for an experienced gardener.

A good way to water

Provided your plant has the proper potting mix and drainage, proceed as follows: 1) Feel the top inch of the soil. If it feels dry to the touch, add tepid water to the soil surface. 2) Continue to add water until you see it seeping from the drainage hole. 3) Allow the plant to drain (either into a sink or drainage tray) for a minimum of ten minutes. 4) Discard any excess water standing in the tray. (A potted plant should never sit in water.) 5) Repeat this procedure when the soil surface again is dry to touch.

Use a watering can with a straight or slightly curved spout (see photograph on page 25). This prevents you from spilling as you water.

After you have followed this watering procedure for a time, you should be able to estimate the amount of water your plants utilize. Add the amount of water each plant uses; then, in a few minutes, check the drainage trays for any excess water.

The soak

Many kinds of house plants, especially Boston ferns, benefit from occasionally having their entire pots

Test moisture level *in potting mix with finger. Add water if soil is dry one inch below soil surface.*

Watering funnel *goes into soil surface; fill with water, then let soak in.*

Immerse *moisture-loving plants pot deep in water-filled pan. Soak plants until the air bubbles stop.*

immersed in water. Soak the pots until bubbles stop coming to the surface; remove the plant and let it drain (see photo page 23). Then return it to its normal place. Immediately after this periodic dunking is a good time to apply fertilizer. Fertilizing is discussed on pages 25-26.

WHEN HUMIDITY IS NEEDED

Most home atmospheres contain a negligible amount of humidity. To a few plant families, such as cactus and succulents, this lack of moisture in the air is unimportant. However, the majority of plants we try to grow indoors originated in tropical jungles, dripping with natural moisture. While a "rain forest" environment is hardly desirable for our homes, the responsibility falls to us to provide some of the humidity our tropical house plants require. Check the Plant Selection Guide (see pages 34-95) to find the humidity needs of your individual plants.

Many factors affect the humidity level inside houses. During the winter months, heating systems reduce natural humidity. Warm summer temperatures also dispel most moisture. The humidity levels in your home can be established with a hygrometer, an instrument that measures moisture present in the air. Inexpensive hygrometers are usually available in hardware stores.

Several methods allow you to increase the humidity in your home: misting your plants; utilizing humidity trays; grouping compatible plants; placing plants in naturally humid areas. These methods, used either individually or in combination, should benefit your moisture-loving plants.

Misting is an easy, inexpensive method of creating a humid atmosphere for your tropical plants. Opinions vary among indoor gardeners on the value of misting plants; daily misting is popular among many orchid and fern lovers, whereas other gardeners mist only occasionally or not at all. Besides creating humidity, misting has the added advantage of cleaning foliage and discouraging pests. To provide humidity for your plants, mist them daily.

Misting should create a fine spray of moisture that surrounds your plant and covers both sides of its leaves. Like watering, misting should be done in the morning so the moisture will have time to evaporate. It's best to let water sit in the mister overnight. Misting does not replace regular watering since the plant absorbs very little of the spray.

If your plant is situated where the spray might damage furniture or other interior surfaces, move the plant to a safe area for misting.

Some hairy-leafed plants, such as African violets, dislike being misted. Water drops on the leaves may cause spotting, especially if the water is below room temperature.

Plastic and metal misters (photo on next page) are available in most nurseries or indoor plant stores. Be sure your mister sprays a fine mist; the plant leaves should look as if a light dew has settled on them and not be dripping wet.

Humidity trays provide for constant water evaporation around house plants. Waterproof trays, large enough to hold one plant or several, are filled with small rocks or pebbles. Add enough water to the tray so the water level remains just below the top of the rocks. The planted container rests on the rocks, preventing it from ever sitting in water. Roots that

Humidity trays: *They keep moisture-loving plants happy*

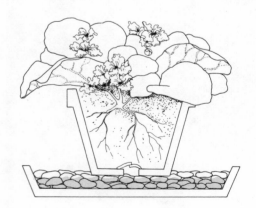 

Two types *of humidity trays you can create: (left) individual saucer filled with small pebbles holds plant so water level never touches pot; (right) large waterproof tray creates humidity for several plants.*

sit constantly in water may rot. This tray will also catch any runoff created during regular watering.

Trays should be constructed of waterproof materials, such as metal, plastic, non-absorbent rubber, or glazed ceramic. Clay saucers absorb and hold moisture that could damage tables, rugs, or other interior surfaces.

Some indoor gardeners create a buffer zone between their humidity trays and floor or furniture surfaces. This prevents any damage caused by condensation. Raising the tray a few inches from the surface forms an air layer to absorb any extra moisture. (Some examples of buffers are on page 14.)

To check the amount of humidity created by this method, hold a hygrometer near the foliage.

Grouping compatible plants is another method of creating humidity indoors. All plants give off water vapor through their leaves in a process called transpiration (this process is described in more detail on pages 4-5). This water vapor creates humidity around each transpiring plant. Grouping plants together lets them share the created humidity.

Besides creating humidity for each other, a group of plants is always more interesting visually than the single parlor palm standing forlornly in a corner.

Naturally humid areas in most homes are the kitchen and the bathroom. The normal activities performed in these rooms, such as dish washing, boiling water, or taking hot showers, create moisture in the air and frequently raise the humidity level.

Moisture-loving plants will thrive in these rooms if their other requirements, such as light and temperature, can also be met.

FERTILIZING HOUSE PLANTS

Many people think that adding fertilizer will feed their plants. This is not precisely true. Plants manufacture their own food by the process of photosynthesis. (Photosynthesis is discussed in detail on page 4.) The fertilizers you provide your house plants assist them in this food production. Most gardeners use the terms "fertilizing" and "feeding" interchangeably.

Plants growing in the ground outdoors can search for the nourishment they need. If their immediate area lacks needed nutrients, the roots can branch into outer areas. A house plant is confined to the soil in its pot; once the nutrients in the potting mix are gone, the plant is stranded. But you can replenish these nutrients by applying fertilizer.

House plant fertilizers usually contain three main nutrients: nitrogen, phosphorus, and potassium or potash. Some fertilizers also include needed trace elements. The ratio of these three ingredients is usually indicated on the label as three numbers, such

Watering and misting tools: *(clockwise from top right) large mister, straight-spouted watering can, brass mister, pressure mister, mister bottle, curved-spout watering can.*

as 5-10-5 or 18-20-16. The first number refers to nitrogen, which stimulates leaf growth and helps leaves maintain a rich green color. The second number indicates phosphorus, which promotes sturdy cell structure and healthy root growth and aids in flower and fruit production. The third number refers to potassium, which aids plants in normal plant functions and development. Choose a fertilizer that indicates it is formulated for house plants; it should be properly balanced in the three main nutrients.

Types of fertilizers

Commercial fertilizers for house plants come in several forms: liquids, powders, tablets, and capsules. Most of these fertilizers are to be dissolved and diluted in water for application. Some types are scratched into the soil surface. Tablets and slow-release capsules are also placed on the soil surface or in the soil. Slow-release fertilizers allow nutrients to be slowly dissolved in normal waterings over a period of time. Whichever type of house plant fertilizer you choose, read the label carefully and follow the directions exactly.

Using fertilizers

Many indoor gardeners find it very beneficial to apply fertilizers more frequently than normal (usually twice as often) but in a very diluted state (usually one-half the recommended dose or less). This provides the plant with nutrients in a more consistent manner.

Fertilizer requirements are given for many common house plants in the Plant Selection Guide on pages 34-95. Know your plant's feeding needs before using any fertilizer.

Never apply fertilizer to dry potting mix. Be sure your plant has been thoroughly watered first.

A newly purchased house plant normally will have been well fed at the nursery or greenhouse and will not need fertilizer for at least three months. A newly repotted plant will find sufficient nutrients in the new potting mix and won't need feeding for a while.

Never fertilize a sick plant. Wait until it has completely recovered before encouraging it to grow.

Most plants rest during the winter months. Don't coax them into growth by applying fertilizer. Most gardeners avoid fertilizers from about September to March. Don't feed dormant plants; wait until they show signs of growth.

Never deliberately overfeed your plants. "An extra pinch to grow on" can damage your plant severely. If you find you have applied too much fertilizer, leaching your plant may wash out some of the excess. (Leaching means watering your plant so water comes out the drainage hole, letting it drain for a while, and then rewatering. Repeat this two or three times.)

Fertilizing through the leaves

Some indoor gardeners have found that spraying fertilizer on plant leaves is helpful to their plants. Plants such as schefflera, philodendron, and Chinese evergreen will respond positively. The leaves become a richer green, perhaps growing a bit in size.

Fertilize by spraying a fine mist of diluted fertilizer with a mister or atomizer until the leaves look as if a good dew has settled on them. Misters and atomizers are illustrated on page 25. Don't leave the foliage dripping wet.

All but the tenderest house plant can benefit from leaf feeding, but be careful not to overfertilize or feed too frequently. If your house plant fertilizer has no instructions for foliar feeding, use it at about half the recommended root feeding strength the first time. Increase the dosage to full strength in successive months.

Foliar feeding does not replace root feeding. Some gardeners root feed at the beginning of each month and then leaf feed at midmonth.

PINCHING AND PRUNING FOR SIZE AND SHAPE

Plant size is an important consideration indoors. Limitations such as ceilings, table tops, and room size indicate the size your house plants should maintain. The solution to the problem of keeping plants to scale is careful pinching and pruning. Pinching encourages bushy growth, whereas pruning reshapes an overgrown plant. Root pruning, though somewhat more drastic, can increase the indoor life of a favorite plant.

One rule to remember: throw out or replace ugly plants. A house plant that has grown too leggy, unwieldy, or misshapen for restorative pruning no longer serves your purpose.

Tip pinching: *The way to make plants bushy*

1. **Leggy plant** *needs to grow bushier, stay more compact in size.*

2. **Pinch out** *growing tip of tallest stem; remove stem close to leaf joint.*

3. **New growth** *forms just below the pinched-out tip, makes plant bushy.*

Fertilize through leaves *by mixing fertilizer, water in mister; spray solution onto plant foliage.*

To knock out *root ball, strike pot on edge of working surface. Support root ball as it slides out.*

Tools for trimming

Although the average gardener requires a wide variety of pruning tools in all shapes and sizes, the indoor gardener needs only a few. The two most generally useful pruning tools are your thumb and forefinger—and these are tools you'll never misplace. They can handle most pinching and pruning on soft-stemmed house plants. Have a sharp knife, a pair of scissors, or commercial hand pruners for the tougher jobs.

Pinching

Like preventive medicine, proper use of the pinching technique avoids more drastic pruning measures. Pinching out the growing tip of a stem promotes side branching that creates thick, bushy plants; pinching stops growth in one direction and redirects it.

Using your thumb and forefinger, pinch out the top growth of a stem or branch. This forces side buds lower on the stem to form new branches. The resulting growth helps form a full well-shaped plant and keeps it from becoming leggy. Tip pinching is illustrated at left.

Pinching should be used on fast-growing, branching plants—such as Swedish ivy, wandering jew, or coleus—that can form new growth on pinched stems. Do not pinch a plant with a single growing stem, such as dracaenas or palms.

Repeat pinching as often as necessary during the plant's growing season. Be sure to pinch only stems that contain at least three or four sets of leaves; these are established and can support new growth.

Prune tree *for shape; remove dead or damaged leaves or branches. Use small hand pruners for job.*

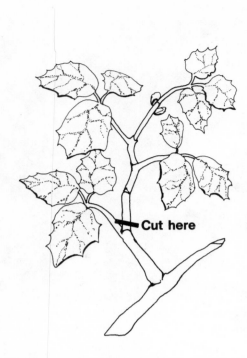

Cut here

Top prune *for plant shape, size. Remove branch as close to leaf joint as possible for appearance.*

Top pruning

Like pinching, top pruning restores the plant's desired shape. Removing leggy growth or branches grown awry improves the plant's appearance and, as with pinching, may encourage new growth.

Cut stems or branches back as far as needed. Use scissors or pruning shears if the stem is too stiff to be pinched off with thumb and forefinger. Always cut just above a leaf node or bud (see the illustration above). Be sure to remove as much of the stem above the node as possible. The node or bud becomes the terminal growing point on the stem, and water and nutrients will travel no farther. The dead or dying stem is useless and could become diseased, endangering your plant.

If you decide to remove a whole branch, cut it off as close to the main stem as possible.

Root pruning

If a plant has reached the maximum size your house can accommodate, consider root pruning. This process takes courage but, if successful, permits your plant to remain in its present container. Root pruning techniques are illustrated at right.

It's best to root prune a plant during a time of active growth, usually in the spring. Have all your materials ready so the procedure can be accomplished as quickly as possible. Remove the plant from its pot (see right for instructions). With a sharp

knife, trim off portions of the root ball on all sides. Cut quickly; do not saw or hack at roots. With plants that have fleshy roots, such as asparagus ferns, chlorophytum, syngonium, or dracaena, severe root pruning could be detrimental. Try washing all the old soil off the roots first. When the root-pruned plant is replaced in its container, there should be about a 1-inch clearance on all sides. Fill in the sides with new potting mix and tamp it in. Water the plant and return it to its place.

A root-pruned plant will revive more quickly if it is also top pruned. See the section on top pruning procedures at left.

REPOTTING PLANTS

Repotting gives house plants a new lease on life. It provides fresh potting mix, more root space to grow into, and a larger foundation for expanding foliage.

While the basic techniques for initial potting and repotting techniques (see pages 16-17) remain the same, the purpose of repotting differs. Initial potting places a newly purchased plant in the container you prefer. Repotting releases an unhappy, potbound plant from a crowded environment and provides a new one.

The potbound plant is a prime candidate for repotting. Symptoms of this malady are roots growing out of the drainage hole, foliage appearing top heavy in a too small pot, stunted growth, and water running quickly through the potting mix with little retention. Roots protruding from the drainage hole or an unbalanced appearance can easily be seen. To check on a watering problem, knock the plant out of its container and examine the root ball to see if the roots are damp.

To knock a plant out of its pot, brace the stem and soil surface with one hand and invert the pot with the other. Strike the pot rim carefully against a solid surface, such as a table top or counter; this should loosen the root ball and allow it to emerge in one piece (see the photograph on page 27). If the root ball refuses to budge after several thumps, run a sharp knife between the pot and root ball.

Once the root ball has been dislodged, examine it closely. If the ball shows mostly potting mix, replace the plant in its pot; being rootbound is not its problem. A root ball that shows mostly tangled roots and very little potting mix, though, needs to be repotted.

To repot your house plant, have all the needed supplies assembled. Quantities of the correct potting mix and the necessary tools should be handy. The new container should be ½ to 1 inch larger in diameter than the plant's present pot.

Be sure to keep the surface of the old root ball on top, filling in around the sides with new potting mix. Most plants adjust poorly to being buried.

Root pruning: *One way to control plant size*

1. Remove root ball *carefully from container. Root pruning permits plant to remain in same container longer.*

2. Cut roots *away carefully, quickly. With a sharp knife, slice, not hack, off portions of root ball.*

3. Replace root ball *on top of enough potting mix to bring plant up to container rim; fill in sides.*

4. Top pruning *allows root-pruned plant to recover more quickly, and reshapes plant's appearance.*

If your plant has problems...

While dusting leaves *gardener can examine plant for possible leaf damage, pests, plant diseases.*

Is your plant sick or unhappy? Brown leaf tips, stunted or abnormal growth, leaves turning yellow and falling off, wilting: these signs and many others signal a plant problem. The culprits can be pests, plant diseases, or, most likely, improper care.

The following chapter gives you guidelines for diagnosing your house plant's problems and corrective measures for solving the problem. One thing you should keep in mind: some plants will be too far gone to be restored to their former appearances. The best approach to these plants is to steel yourself to discard them. There is nothing attractive or appealing about a sickly plant, and its problem might spread to its companions.

PREVENT TROUBLE BEFORE IT HAPPENS

Although no indoor plant is immune from problems, pests, or plant diseases, taking simple precautions will reduce the chance of its experiencing a setback in development. Most of the following preventive measures are discussed elsewhere in this book, but they are worth repeating:

1) Always use clean plant containers and sterilized potting mix when planting or transplanting to give your house plants a fresh start.

2) Carefully examine plants before bringing them home to be sure they are free of pests and diseases.

3) Isolate new house plants for a few weeks (if you have adequate space) to be sure they are healthy and free of pests and diseases before adding them to your plant collection.

4) Look up each house plant in the Plant Selection Guide on pages 34-95 to study its growing requirements. (Most common house plants are listed in this guide.) Try to provide your plant with as many of its needs as possible.

5) Develop the habit of the routine inspection as described on pages 20-21.

6) If you find a sick plant in your home, isolate it from other house plants until it is cured. This helps prevent pests or disease from spreading.

COMMON PLANT PROBLEMS

Most house plant problems you find will be the result of improper care. And, like most problems, the cause is rarely a simple one. Poor indoor gardening habits, a bad growing location, or a combination of the two can cause various reactions in your plant's appearance. Treat these reactions as a call for help; left without aid, your house plant may die.

This section lists plant problems by the effect each problem has on a plant's appearance, offers possible causes, and suggests methods for correction. Study each plant's problem carefully; try to diagnose and treat it as quickly as possible. If you are unsure of how to correct a problem, refer to the appropriate section of this book.

Leaf tips and leaf margins turn brown from improper plant care. Overwatering or underwatering, too much sun or heat through a window, too much fertilizer, watering with a water high in salt concentration, not enough humidity, locating the plant in drafts, or a combination of these care problems may result in browned tips or margins. Study your plant's situation to try and locate the possible cause. Then remedy it. If the cause isn't easily discernible, try eliminating each possibility, one at a time.

Yellowing leaves on house plants have a variety of possible causes. Not enough light or too much light and lack of fertilizer or too much fertilizer are common problems. Yellowing leaves may also be the result of a high nighttime temperature or too much water. Sucking insects (probably scale insects or mealybugs) on plant stems between the yellowing leaves and the roots are another possible cause. Study the care you give your plant to locate the cause of the yellowing foliage. The green color may or may not return to the damaged leaves after the problem is corrected.

Leaf drop can be caused by one or a combination of several problems. Overwatering or underwatering, too much sun, too much fertilizer, not enough humidity, or leaving your plant in a drafty location can cause leaves to drop. If only the lower leaves drop, your plant probably needs more light. Once leaves have fallen off because of improper care, they seldom grow back. However, you can save the plant by correcting the cause of the problem.

Wilting is a normal plant reaction to too much sun or heat, too much or not enough water, or a poor growing location. Try moving the plant to a better spot and check your watering techniques. Plants that need water will perk up quickly from a needed drink. This process isn't detrimental to the plant as long as it isn't allowed to wilt too frequently.

Dry and brittle leaves may mean your plant isn't getting enough water or the humidity levels are too low.

Review your watering practices. Try regular misting or place the plant on a humidity tray (humidity trays are discussed on page 24).

Leggy growth is caused by not providing your house plant with enough light. Try moving it to a location with more light and pinch back the leggy stems.

Brown or yellow spots on leaf edges or surfaces are unsightly and indicate too much water, too much direct sun, or a drafty location. Check the plant's present situation and make the needed corrections.

No flowers on a normally flowering house plant may be caused by a variety of conditions. Not enough light or room temperatures that remain too high at nighttime are possible causes. Try moving your blooming plant to a well-lighted spot. Check the nighttime temperature of its new location; if the temperature is too high, find a well-lighted, cool spot or move the plant each evening to a cool area.

Flower buds drop off for many reasons. Possible causes are inadequate light or too much sun, low room temperature, improper watering habits, or not enough fertilizer. Check your house plant's individual situation to pinpoint the problem.

Soft stem bases on house plants usually indicate rot. Overwatering is probably the culprit. Watch your watering habits carefully.

Soggy soil is the result of overwatering and/or improper drainage. Knock out the root ball (see pages 28-29) to check the drainage problem; make sure the drainage hole isn't plugged. If overwatering created the problem, try to restrain that heavy hand when it's time to water.

KNOW YOUR PESTS

Indoor pests are small, sometimes almost microscopic. You may not be aware of the little creatures until your favorite plant takes a turn for the worse. The routine inspection, discussed on pages 20-21, should nip most pest problems in the bud. If you do find pests, eradicate them as quickly as possible. Plants do not always recover even if all the pests are destroyed.

There are two approaches to pest control: one is direct, involving physical removal of the pests; the other requires using pesticides, which is less direct and not always beneficial to the plant.

The direct approach is to remove pests by hand or to wash them off with water from a hose or under a water faucet. Some gardeners have been successful using a mist sprayer. An advantage this approach offers is that it can be repeated as often as needed to control pests. Most insecticides require a certain waiting period between doses. The chief problem

Fuzzy, white mealybugs *like to hide on underside of leaves at joint; are difficult to detect quickly.*

with this method is that you might miss eliminating insect eggs in the soil.

Spraying plants with insecticides can be almost as harmful to some house plants as the pest infestation itself. Always read and carefully follow the directions on the label of all pesticides. Be sure the insecticide will effectively eliminate the specific pest attacking your plant and that it is recommended for use on house plants. If you use a spray specifically formulated for house plants, be sure it is recommended for use on your particular plant. Some tender plants, such as ferns, may succumb to the spray itself. It's best to spray plants outdoors. When you do, any spray residue will be dispersed outside in the open air, and you can be sure to cover leaf surfaces, both top and bottom, without worrying about damaging furniture surfaces. The pushbutton containers of house plant insecticides are best for the indoor gardener, both in ease and economy. Other types of sprays need to be mixed, a time-consuming and messy process that requires special equipment, and these insecticides are only available in large quantities.

Your first step is to identify your plant problem as a pest infestation. Some pests, such as mealy bugs or aphids, will be visible on the plant or in the container; others, too small for visual identification, can also cause extensive plant damage. Once you've determined a pest problem, isolate the infected plant immediately to prevent infection of other plants. The following section contains information on identifying each house plant pest, the plant damage they create, and the various methods of eliminating them.

Aphids

Aphids have soft, round or pear-shaped bodies, usually green, reddish, or black. They may have wings. They tend to cluster on buds or on new plant growth.

Plant damage. Aphids suck plant juices, causing poor growth, stunted plants, or curled, distorted leaves or flowers. Their honeydew secretions give leaves a shiny appearance and may form a base for the growth of a sooty mold.

Control. Wash aphids off with water from a hose, with a mist sprayer, or in a soapy (*not* detergent) solution. Pyrethrum or rotenone can also be used.

Mealybugs

Although large enough to be spotted easily, mealybugs normally cluster on leaf stems or in branch crotches out of the light, making them difficult to detect. They have round, white, fuzzy-looking bodies· (See the photograph at left.)

Plant damage. Like sucking insects, mealybugs cause stunted growth, eventually killing house plants. They also secrete a honeydew that gives leaves a shiny, sticky surface and forms a base on which black mold can grow.

Control. Remove mealybugs by touching them with a cotton swab dipped in alcohol, washing them off with water from a hose or a spray mister, or spraying them with petroleum oils.

Scale insects

Scale exists in many varieties. Usually brown or gray-colored with a round or oval-shaped body, scale insects have a hard-shell covering in their adult stage. Some types attack plant leaves; others attack stems. They can be especially difficult to detect on fern fronds because they resemble spores. (See the photograph on next page, bottom left.)

Plant damage. Scales are sucking insects that use plant juices for food. They cause stunted or poor plant growth. They also secrete honeydew that gives leaves a shiny, sticky surface and forms a base for the growth of sooty mold.

Control. Scrape off scale insects with your fingernail or with a small knife or wash them off in a soapy water solution. Lime sulfur or petroleum oils are also effective in controlling scale for some plants; read the container label.

Spider mites

A common house plant pest, the spider mite is so small that it is only detectable in groups or by the characteristic webbing it leaves on plant foliage. Mites have flat, oval bodies, usually white or red. (See the photograph on next page, bottom right.)

Plant damage. Leaves may yellow and die or fall off. Some leaves become mottled with brown or yellow spots. Leaf undersides are covered with a fine webbing. Infected plants become stunted and may die.

Control. Isolate infected plants at once. Spider mites spread like wildfire. Wash off with water from a hose or in a soapy solution. Lime sulfur, dusting sulfur, or petroleum oils are also effective. Regular misting also helps to control mites.

Thrips

Very small and fast-moving, thrips are barely visible. They have slender bodies in colors of tan, browns, or black, with lighter-colored markings. When disturbed, they may fly or leap.

Plant damage. Thrips feed on foliage or flowers, causing distorted growth of the plant tissue. Their rasping damage is sometimes visible on stems or leaf edges.

Control. Wash thrips off with water from a hose or with a mist sprayer. Apply pyrethrum, rotenone, or petroleum oils.

Whiteflies

These common pests, found both indoors and out, are very small and have white bodies and wings. They flutter about plants in a white cloud when the plant they're attacking is disturbed. The young attach themselves to the underside of leaves.

Plant damage. Attacked leaves turn a pale color. The foliage surface is covered with a shiny, sticky layer of honeydew. The honeydew forms a base on which sooty molds can grow.

Control. Wash whiteflies off with water from a hose or with a mist sprayer. Apply pyrethrum, rotenone, or petroleum oil to the infected plant. Whiteflies may require several applications.

PLANT DISEASES

For house plants to develop diseases is rather uncommon. Most disease problems result from poor growing conditions, improper care, or purchasing an already diseased plant. Carefully examine a plant for signs of disease before purchasing it; guidelines are given on page 9.

Crown or root rot are usually caused by poor drainage and overwatering. Plants may turn brown or suddenly wilt. If the plant isn't too far gone, transplanting may be beneficial. Correcting your watering habits should avoid a recurrence of this disease.

Mildew appears on plant leaves, stems, or flower buds as a white or gray powder. Leaves may curl or be distorted. Overwatering and poor air circulation are probable causes. Try moving the infected plant to a better location, correct your watering habits, and, if necessary, spray the infected plant with sulfur dust or benomyl.

Scale insects *are flat, latch onto undersides of leaves, stems. This plant has a heavy infestation.*

Spider mites *are minute. Infestation is characterized by fine webbing, yellow-mottled foliage.*

Plant selection guide

This comprehensive guide offers you a list of common plants that can be successfully grown indoors. The plants described as "indoor-outdoor plants" can be brought indoors periodically to enjoy but are primarily suited to be grown outdoors.

Many of these house plants are pictured to better help you locate and identify them. Most of the plants listed can be found in various sized containers in nurseries, indoor plant boutiques, or florist shops.

Plants are listed alphabetically by their botanical names. Common name listings will direct you to the botanical name listing that gives you a description of the plant's appearance and growth habits, its care requirements, and other related varieties that also make suitable house plants.

ABUTILON. Flowering maple, Chinese lantern. Tropical plant from South America grown for its globe-shaped flowers that can bloom year around. Pinch constantly to control growth and extend bloom. Can be grown upright or trained to hang. Needs at least 4 hours full sun daily and likes regular fertilizing and standard potting mix kept moist (See photo, page 35 top.)

A. hybridum. Bell-shaped flowers come in white, pink, yellow, and red. The best-known flowering maple.

A. megapotamicum. Weeping Chinese lantern. Drooping growth good for hanging baskets. Flowers red and yellow.

A. striatum thompsonii. Variegated foliage, green with creamy yellow; flowers are pale orange veined with red.

ACALYPHA hispida. Chenille plant, Red-hot cattail. Nicknames come from long, tassel-like red or purple blooms. Has bright green, hairy leaves. Needs heavy pruning to control size. Provide bright light, humidity; keep potting mix moist but not soggy. *Acalypha* hates wet feet. Fertilize during growing season. Use standard potting mix.

ACHIMENES. Tropical American plant that grows from rhizomes. Best used in hanging baskets. Flowers in blue, pink, yellow, red, purple. Needs bright light (no direct sun), temperatures above 60°, potting

Buying a plant? *Be a wise shopper; know the type of house plant you want and the care it will require.*

mix kept evenly moist during growing season, fertilize during blooming season. To grow: Plant rhizomes March-April, placing ½-1 inch deep in moist peat moss and sand. Keep in light shade at 60° with constant moisture. When growth is 3 inches, plant in standard potting mix. In fall, dry rhizomes and let soil dry out; store in cool dry spot; repot in spring and resume watering. (See photo at right.)

ACORUS gramineus variegatus. Miniature sweet flag, Japanese sweet flag. Grass-like native of Japan with green and white foliage. Likes standard potting mix, lots of water, medium to bright light, high humidity, and temperatures around 55°. Good in terrariums. Plants should not touch container sides.

    A. g. pusillus. A dwarf variety with flat, dark green leaves.

ADIANTUM raddianum (*A. cuneatum*). Maidenhair fern. Wiry, black stems hold lacy, bright green, fan-shaped leaflets. Plants need potting mix high in organic matter, shade (north or sunless window), steady moisture (never let roots dry out), good drainage, high humidity (likes misting), cool temperatures preferably below 65°. Mature fronds die back but new ones soon appear. Cut out dead fronds for appearance. Can be moved outdoors to a shaded patio for summer. Is considered difficult to grow.

ADROMISCHUS maculatus. Calico hearts. A succulent with gray-green, thick, flat leaves, spotted brown. Plant rarely blooms indoors. Needs at least 4 hours of sun; let potting mix dry out completely between waterings. Plant in ½ standard potting mix, ½ sharp sand.

AECHMEA. Bromeliad that grows in the vase form. Plant in a fast-draining but moisture-retentive potting mix. Likes bright light (no hot sun), regular fertilizing. Water when soil is really dry to touch; fill vase with water. (See photo at right.)

    A. chantinii. Olive to brownish green leaves barred with silver. Flower cluster has yellow blooms; orange, red, or pink bracts tipped yellow and white.

    A. fasciata. Green leaves banded white with a powdery surface. Flower cluster begins blue, changes to deep rose with age. Bracts are pink.

    A. 'Foster's Favorite'. Wine red, lacquered leaves. Flowers on drooping, spikelike clusters in coral red and blue.

    A. fulgens discolor. Green leaves backed with purple. Flowers are red tipped in blue; rose-colored berries follow.

    A. 'Royal Wine'. Dark green leaves backed with dark wine color. Flowers deep orange tipped in blue.

AEONIUM. Decorative succulent with leaves in rosettes. Likes good light, air circulation. Water when potting mix feels dry to touch. (Be sure roots are dry). Plant in ½ standard potting mix, ½ sharp sand.

Abutilon

Achimenes

Aechmea chantinii

Aeschynanthus lobbianus

Aeschynanthus marmoratus

Agave

A. arboreum atropurpureum. Dark maroon leaves.
A. canariense. Apple green leaves.

AERIDES. Epiphytic orchids from tropical Asia that can become quite tall. Plants have central stem with fleshy green leaves. Flower spikes hold closely-set, fragrant, waxy flowers in summer. Likes bright light, humidity. Needs ample water spring, summer; less the rest of year.
A. crassifolium. To 10 inches; amethyst purple flowers.
A. multiflorum. White and purple summer flowers.
A. odoratum. To 40 inches; 1-inch flowers are white mottled with purple. Spicy fragrance.

AESCHYNANTHUS (Trichosporum). Basketvine. Shining leaves usually in pairs on drooping stems; good in hanging baskets. Tubular flowers. Prefers warm temperatures, high humidity, regular fertilizing, good light. Keep potting mix moist but not soggy. Plant in loose, open, fibrous potting mix. (See photos at left.)
A. lobbianus. Lipstick vine. Red, 2-inch tubular flowers emerge from calyces like lipsticks from cases.
A. marmoratus. Zebra basket vine. Green foliage mottled with maroon. Green tubular flowers.
A. speciosus. Yellow and orange flowers up to 4 inches long.

AFRICAN VIOLET. See Saintpaulia ionantha.

AGAPANTHUS. Lily-of-the-Nile. Large container plant that can summer outdoors. Grow evergreen varieties in sunny window in standard potting mix. Likes lots of water during growing season. Keep potbound for good bloom.
A. africanus (often sold as *A. umbellatus*). Evergreen. Most common variety. Flower stalks to 1½ feet. Blue or white flowers midsummer to fall.
A. 'Dwarf White'. Evergreen. Foliage to 1-1½ feet. White flowers on stalks 1½-2 feet tall.
A. 'Peter Pan'. Evergreen dwarf variety. Foliage clumps 8-12 inches tall. Blue flowers on 12-18-inch stems.

AGAVE. Century plant. Use smaller varieties indoors. Succulent that prefers a sunny window, warm temperatures; let potting mix dry out completely between waterings. Plant in ½ standard potting mix, ½ sharp sand. Fertilize infrequently to keep compact. (See photo at left.)
A. filifera. Thread Agave. Narrow, olive green leaves with loose, curled threads at margins.
A. picta. Narrow, pale green leaves with white margins, small black teeth.
A. victoriae-reginae. Olive green leaves with white lines.

AGLAONEMA. Hardy tropical with graceful oblong leaves, variegated on some types. Likes standard potting mix, warm temperatures, good light, frequent waterings, but adaptable to poor light and low moisture. Great for poorly lighted situations. Small greenish flowers resemble callas. Cuttings will grow a long time in plain water. Exudation from leaf tips, especially from *A. modestum*, spots wood finishes. (See photo at right.)

A. commutatum. Deep green leaves with pale green markings. Variety 'White Rajah' has white markings.

A. modestum. Chinese evergreen. Shiny, dark green leaves.

A. roebelinii. Leathery leaves marked with pale green.

A. treubii. Bluish-green leaves marked with silver. Plant grows to 10 inches.

AIR PLANT. See Kalanchoe pinnata.

ALLAMANDA cathartica 'Hendersonii'. Green-leafed climber bears fragrant, golden, tubular flowers. Prune to keep compact. Give at least 4 hours of sun, around 50% humidity, lots of water and regular fertilizing during growing season.

ALOE. Easy-to-grow succulent of the lily family, mostly from South Africa. Forms clumps of fleshy, pointed leaves with clusters of orange, yellow, or red flowers. Plant in well drained soil; likes a sunny window, can tolerate less. Let soil dry between waterings; be sure to soak plants thoroughly.

A. nobilis. Pointed, dark green leaves edged with irregular white teeth; rosette form on a short stem. Flowers orange-red. Takes limited root space.

A. striata. Coral aloe. Stiff pointed leaves, gray green with narrow pinkish edge; rosette form on short stem.

A. variegata. Partridge-breast aloe, tiger aloe. Wavy bands of white markings on green leaves. Flowers pink to dull red.

A. vera. Pale green leaves with hard spines, upright growth to 12 inches. Sap used medicinally as a home remedy for burns.

ALUMINUM PLANT. See Pilea cadierei.

AMARYLLIS. See Hippeastrum.

ANANAS. Pineapple. Bromeliad that may bear fruit indoors. Can be grown from leafy top of commercial pineapple: cut off top, remove any flesh, and let dry for a week in a shady spot; peel off any dried lower leaves and plant. Likes standard potting mix, good light, temperatures above 68°. Water when soil dry. Fertilize every 3-4 weeks. (See photo at right.)

A comosus. Stiff, spiny, dark green leaves; produces edible fruit.

A. nanas. Most common pineapple. Gray-green leaves. Produces fruit.

ANGEL'S TEARS. See Soleirolia soleirolii.

ANGRAECUM. Epiphytic orchids from Asia and Ceylon. Starlike white or greenish white flowers in

Aglaonema treubii

Ananas

Aphelandra squarrosa

Araucaria heterophylla

winter. Plant in fir bark or osmunda. Keep constantly moist all year except fall when soil should dry out between waterings. Likes bright light.

A. eburneum. Grows to 48 inches. Three-inch, waxy greenish white flowers.

A. sesquipedale. Grows to 36 inches. Bears fragrant, 6-inch, ivory white flowers, each with 10-inch spur. Likes nighttime temperatures of 55°.

ANTHURIUM. Exotic perennial native to tropical America. Shiny, dark green leaves with lustrous flower bracts in red, pink, white. No more difficult to grow indoors than some orchids. Likes high humidity, 50% or above. Keep plants on humidity trays; mist leaves several times daily. Give good light but not direct sun. Grows best in 80°-90° temperatures but adaptable to less; growth stops if temperature drops below 65°. Keep out of drafts. Plant in a coarse, porous mix of leaf mold, sandy soil, and shredded osmunda. Give ample water at room temperature. Fertilize with a mild feeding every 4 weeks.

A. andraeanum. Dark green, oblong leaves to 1 foot long, 6 inches wide. Flower bracts red, rose, pink, or white shine as though lacquered. Yellow, callalike flower spike. Blooms will last 6 weeks on plant—4 weeks cut.

A. scherzerianum. Flamingo flower. Dwarf form grows slowly to 2 feet. Flower bracts vary from deep red through salmon to white. Yellow flower spikes spirally coiled.

APHELANDRA squarrosa. Native to Mexico, South America. Showy, dark green, waxy leaves with white veins; large yellow flower clusters. Requires diffused light or morning sun, standard potting mix, 50°-70° temperatures, high humidity; routine watering. Prune plants to keep compact. To make plants bushy, cut stems back to one or two pairs of leaves after flowering. (See photo at left.)

A. s. 'Brockfeld'. Grows compactly with broader leaves than 'Louisae'. Leaves glossy black with straw yellow veining.

A. s. 'Dania'. Most compact in growth.

A. s. 'Louisae'. Best known variety.

APOSTLE PLANT. See Neomarica northiana.

ARALIA elegantissima. See Dizygotheca elegantissima.

ARALIA SIEBOLDII. See Fatsia japonica.

ARAUCARIA heterophylla *(A. excelsa)*. Norfolk Island pine. Slow growing evergreen with pyramidal form; can reach 12 feet indoors. Branches grow in tiers. Can be kept in container for many years; can double as indoor Christmas tree. May be summered outdoors; keep out of hot sun. Likes cool temperatures, good light, standard potting mix. Don't crowd; it needs good air circulation. Need lots of water, good drainage. (See photo at left.)

ARDISIA crenata (*A. crenulata, A. crispa*). Coral berry. Native of China and Malaysia, usually grown as a single stem with long, shiny, dark green leaves. Thrives with standard potting mix, diffused light, ample water, regular fertilizing, and high humidity. In spring, white or pinkish flower clusters followed by scarlet berries that last into winter. Grows slowly to about 18 inches.

ARROWHEAD PLANT. See Syngonium podophyllum.

ARTILLERY PLANT. See Pilea microphylla.

ASPARAGUS, ORNAMENTAL. Asparagus fern. Not a true fern but has the same feathery qualities. Fast grower. Thrives in standard potting mix with peat moss or ground bark added. Provide adequate drainage. Likes good light, ample water; can tolerate less. Leaves will turn yellow in inadequate light. Does not require as much humidity as true fern but likes frequent misting. Red spider mites common pests. (See photos at right.)

A. asparagoides 'Myrtifolius'. Baby smilax. Has broad glossy "leaves." Can be a hanger.

A. densiflorus 'Myeri' (*A. meyeri*). Plume asparagus, Foxtail asparagus. Stiff, upright stems densely covered with tiny needles.

A. d. 'Sprengeri' (*A. sprengeri*). Sprenger asparagus. Most common variety. Hardy grower with drooping stems. Good as a hanger. Mature form has tiny, pinkish flowers followed by coral-red berries.

A. falcatus. Sickle-thorn asparagus. Has glossy leaves, curved thorns on stems. White flowers followed by brown berries. Fast growing.

A. retrofractus. Ming fern. Erect, shrubby. Slender zigzag, silvery gray stems; threadlike leaves in fluffy, rich green tufts. Clusters of small white flowers.

A. setaceus (*A. plumosus*). Hardy plant with delicate feathery appearance. Dark green foliage. Commonly used by florists as fillers in bouquets. Dwarf version called 'Nanus'.

ASPIDISTRA elatior (*A. lurida*). Cast-iron plant. Sturdy, long-lived foliage plant with a strong constitution. Tough, glossy, dark green leaves, 1-2½ feet long, 3-4 inches wide. Although tolerant of a variety of conditions, prefers high humidity, cool temperatures, standard potting mix kept constantly moist, and fertilizing in spring and summer. Light can range from dark shade to filtered sun. Keep leaves dust-free by washing with a hose or cleaning with a soft cloth. The variegated form (*A. e. 'Variegata'*) has leaves striped with white, loses variegation if planted in soil that is too rich. (See photo at right.)

ASPLENIUM. Spleenwort. Widespread, variable group of graceful hardy ferns. Plant in standard potting mix and give lots of water. Be sure drainage is good. Likes high humidity (use humidity trays),

Asparagus densiflorus 'Myeri'

Asparagus densiflorus 'Sprengeri'

Aspidistra elatior

Asplenium bulbiferum

Asplenium nidus

good sunless light as in north window. Plants may turn brown in winter if humidity is excessive. (See photos at left.)

A. bulbiferum. Mother fern, Mother spleenwort. Native to Malaysia, New Zealand. Upward growth of feathery, bright green fronds may reach 4 feet. Forms tiny new plantlets on fronds that can be removed and planted. Likes frequent misting.

A. nidus. Bird's-nest fern. Showy, apple green, undivided fronds with black rib unfurl from heart of plant. Can be summered outdoors on a shady patio. Water accumulation in heart may cause crown rot. Fronds dislike being touched.

ASTROPHYTUM. Cactus native to Mexico. Likes warm temperatures, good air circulation. Plant in equal parts standard potting mix and sharp sand. Water when potting mix dries out completely.

A. capricorne. Goat's horn. Green globe with silver markings. Yellow, 3-inch flowers with red throats.

A. myriostigma. Bishop's cap. Gray-ribbed, spineless globe; yellow flowers.

A. ornatum. Star cactus. Ribbed plants either globe or column. Spines, flowers yellow.

AUCUBA japonica. Japanese aucuba. Asian shrub native from Himalayas to Japan, has shiny, oval, green leaves. Likes high humidity, cool temperatures, and light from north window. Use standard potting mix and give ample water. Regular misting discourages pests. Can be summered outdoors; protect from hot sun. Prune to keep small.

A. j. 'Crotonifolia'. Leaves heavily splashed with white and gold splotches.

A. j. 'Variegata'. Gold dust plant. Yellow spots on dark green leaves.

AZALEA. Indoor-outdoor plant. Relative of rhododendron. Popular gift plant, usually with forced blooms. Bring indoors while flowering for color. Flowers in reds, pinks, white or variegated. Give bright light, high humidity and cool nighttime temperatures. Use fast-draining soil and keep moist. When flowers fade, prune; then place outdoors after frost danger is gone (forced plants are tender). Feed with acid plant food every 6-8 weeks, 3 or 4 times from end of bloom until September. Pinch new tips to keep bushy.

AZTEC COLUMN. See Cephalocereus polyanthus.

BABY SMILAX. See Asparagus asparagoides myrtifolius.

BABY'S TEARS. See Pilea depressa, Soleirolia soleirolii.

BALL FERN. See Davallia bullata mariesii.

BALSAM. See Impatiens walleriana.

BAMBOO. Giant grasses with woody stems. Indoor-outdoor plants. See *Bambusa multiplex riviereorum, Phyllostachys, Sasa palmata.*

BAMBURANTA. See Ctenanthe compressa.

BAMBUSA multiplex riviereorum. Chinese goddess bamboo. Indoor-outdoor plant. Graceful, dense, clump growth to 4-6 feet. Needs wide space to show off properly. Not recommended for year-round indoor culture but can spend extended periods indoors in containers. Give cool temperatures, bright light. To restrain growth, keep potting mix on the dry side. Fertilize regularly and repot every 2-3 years. When moving indoors or out, avoid sudden changes in light, temperature.

BANANA. See Musa.

BASEBALL PLANT. See Euphorbia obesa.

BASKET VINE. See Aeschynanthus.

BEAD PLANT. See Nertera granadensis.

BEAR'S FOOT FERN. See Humata tyermannii.

BEAUCARNEA recurvata (*Nolina*). Elephant-foot tree, Pony tail. Hardy, palmlike. Grows vigorously indoors. Only barrier is ceiling height. Move outdoors when too large. A conversation piece, palm has bulbous trunk base resembling an elephant's foot. Crown of leaves tops trunk. Likes warm, dry atmosphere. Water only when potting mix completely dry.

BEAVER TAIL. See Opuntia basilaris.

BEGONIA. Huge group of plants, most of which make superb house plants. Generally prefer filtered light, regular fertilizing, rich potting mix that is slightly acid (add peat moss, leaf mold, or organic matter to standard potting mix). Keep plants constantly moist with perfect drainage. Below is a partial list of terms and plant kinds you may encounter. (See photos at right, and page 42.)

Angel-wing begonias. Cane-stemmed begonias with pairs of leaves that resemble extended wings.

Cane-stemmed begonias. Fibrous-rooted begonias with jointed stems with bamboolike joints. Growth erect or spreading. Includes angel-wing begonias.

B. 'Corallina de Lucerna' ('Lucerna'). Angel-wing. Leaves are silver spotted. Clusters of coral flowers. Likes strong light but not hot sun. Keep soil constantly moist. Prune hard after flowering to keep bushy.

Elatior begonias. Recently introduced. Winter blooming with single red, red-orange, and pink on upright plants; double red, rose, pink flowers on sprawling plants. Like good light but not hot sun. Water when top inch of potting mix is dry to touch. Keep water off leaves to prevent mildew. Fertilize sparingly for good bloom. Summer bloom can be forced by putting plant in dark room to create longer nights.

B. 'Erythrophylla' (*B. 'Feastii'*). Beefsteak begonia. Rhizomatous. Round, 2-3 inch leaves, dark green top, deep red below. Pink flowers.

Begonia, Angel-wing

Begonia, Elatior

Begonia masoniana

Begonia rex-cultorum

Fibrous-rooted begonias. Begonias that grow from masses of fibrous roots. Mostly easy to grow.

B. fuchsioides. Fibrous-rooted. Small, bright green, shiny leaves; drooping clusters of pink or red flowers. Erect stems arching at tips.

B. masoniana. Iron cross begonia. Rhizomatous. Big, rough, chartreuse green leaves centered with a brown marking that resembles a Maltese or German cross. Insignificant white flowers with dark bristles.

B. rex-cultorum. Rex begonia. Many varieties with magnificently colored, shieldlike leaves. Leaf colors in maroon, lilac, rose, greens, silvery gray, and combinations. Don't overfeed or overwater. Give good light, no hot sun. May go dormant in winter.

Rhizomatous begonias. Begonias that form a rhizome (a thick, short stem, usually creeping, sometimes underground). Don't overfeed or overwater; the rhizome serves as a sort of emergency canteen that sustains plants through adversity. Give good light, no hot sun. May go dormant in winter; keep on the dry side until new growth resumes.

B. semperflorens. Wax begonia. Fibrous-rooted dwarf (4-6 inches), best indoors. Leaves bright green, bronzy, or reddish, some with reddish ribs. Flowers, single or double, in white, red, rose, pinks. Can take sun if well watered. Calla lily begonias are a kind of *B. semperflorens* with some foliage variegated with white. Rather delicate. Give cool temperatures, bright light (no hot sun), high humidity. Avoid overwatering.

BELLFLOWER, Italian. See Campanula.

BELOPERONE guttata. Shrimp plant. Native to Mexico. Indoor-outdoor plant. Apple green, oval leaves; tubular flowers are white, purple-spotted, enclosed in copper bronze, with overlapping bracts resembling large shrimp. Constant pinching needed to keep plant bushy, compact. Likes at least 4 hours of sun daily (outdoors in summer, grow in partial shade; bracts and foliage fade in too much sun), standard potting mix, regular fertilizing, high humidity. Water when soil surface is almost dry; too much or too little water may cause leaf drop.

BERMUDA BUTTERCUP. See Oxalis pes-caprae.

BIFRENARIA. Epiphytic orchid from Brazil. Dark green, leathery leaves, showy flowers. Likes sun or bright light. Plant in fir bark or osmunda. Rest plants without water for a month after they bloom.

B. harrisoniae. Three-inch, creamy white flowers with reddish purple lip. Spring blooming.

BILLBERGIA. Epiphytic bromeliad native to Brazil. Stiff, spiny-toothed leaves in rosette form. Long-lasting tubular flowers on long, arching stems. Plant in equal parts sharp sand and fir bark or leaf mold. Likes bright light (can take morning sun), regular fertilizing, warm temperatures. Mist frequently. Keep vase at center of leaf rosette filled with water.

Needs lots of water during growth, much less in winter.

B. nutans. Queen's tears. Leaves green with silver cast. Flowers chartreuse-green tipped in violet red, bracts rose red.

B. pyramidalis. Large plant. Leaves to 3 feet long. Flowers red, violet-tipped, red bracts.

B. sanderiana. Leathery leaves to 1 foot dotted white. Large flower cluster; flowers blue, yellowish green at base; rose-colored bracts.

BIRD OF PARADISE. See Strelitzia reginae.

BIRD'S-NEST FERN. See Asplenium nidus.

BISHOP'S CAP. See Astrophytum myriostigma.

BLEEDING HEART. See Clerodendrum thomsoniae.

BLOOD-LEAF. See Iresine herbstii.

BOSTON FERN. See Nephrolepis exaltata 'Bostoniense'.

BOUGAINVILLEA. Indoor-outdoor plant. Evergreen. Colorful bracts. Use shrub varieties indoors. Provide supports for vining. Likes at least 4 hours of sun daily, average to warm temperatures, standard potting mix, regular fertilizing. Water well during growth; ease off temporarily at midsummer for better flowering. Prune for shape. Be careful when repotting not to disturb the roots. Some varieties: 'Convent' ('Panama Queen'), magenta-purple bracts; 'Crimson Jewel', red bracts; 'La Jolla', red bracts; 'Temple Fire', bronze red bracts. (See photo at right.)

BOWSTRING HEMP. See Sansevieria.

BOX-LEAF EUONYMUS. See Euonymus japonica 'Microphylla'.

BOXWOOD. See Buxus microphylla japonica.

BRASSAIA actinophylla *(Shefflera actinophylla).* Queensland umbrella tree, Octopus tree, Umbrella plant. Shiny, oval, pointed leaves; 7-16 leaflets held on long stems; leaves radiate outward like umbrella ribs. Can become large. Needs room to show form. Likes standard potting mix, occasional fertilizing, bright light; plants can tolerate adverse conditions. Let potting mix dry completely between waterings. Frequent misting keeps leaves clean, discourages pests. (See photo at right.)

BRASSAVOLA. Epiphytic orchid native to tropical America. Tough, leathery, green leaves grow from pseudobulbs. Large, spiderlike flowers in white or greenish white. Plant in packaged orchid potting mix. Needs 60°-65° nighttime temperatures, high humidity, at least 4 hours of sun daily during growing season. Keep potting mix constantly moist except during dormancy. Reduce humidity during dormant period.

B. cucullata. Fragrant, 2-inch flowers bloom summer, fall.

Bougainvillea

Brassaia actinophylla

Buxus microphylla japonica

Caladium bicolor

B. nodosa. Lady-of-the-Night. Three-inch flowers in fall, sweetly fragrant at night. Grows best in hanging containers.

BRASSIA maculata. Spider orchid. Large epiphytic orchids found from Mexico to Brazil and Peru. Leaves grow from pseudobulbs. Spiderlike, whitish green and brown flowers are fragrant, bloom in early summer. Plant in fir bark or osmunda. Needs sun, warm temperatures (over 60°). Keep potting mix constantly moist throughout year.

BROMELIAD. Any plant that belongs to the bromelia or pineapple family *(Bromeliaceae)*. Most bromeliads are stemless perennials with clustered leaves and with showy flowers in simple or branched clusters with colorful bracts. Leaves of many kinds are handsomely marked. Most kinds grown indoors are epiphytes, plants that perch in trees or rocks and gain their sustenance from rain and leaf mold gathering around their roots. These often have cupped leaf bases or "vases" that hold water between rains. For bromeliads that will grow indoors, see: *Aechmea, Ananas, Billbergia, Cryptanthus zonatus, Dyckia fosteriana, Guzamania lingulata, Neoregelia, Nidularium innocentii, Tillandsia lindeniana, Vriesia.*

BUNNY EARS. See Opuntia microdasys.

BURRO TAIL. See Sedum morganianum.

BUSY LIZZIE. See Impatiens walleriana.

BUTTERFLY ORCHID. See Oncidium papilio.

BUTTON FERN. See Pellaea rotundifolia.

BUXUS microphylla japonica. Japanese boxwood. Miniature, small-leafed, slow-growing, evergreen shrub. Foliage a rich green. Good plant for dish gardens. Likes standard potting mix, at least 4 hours of sun daily, cool temperatures. Water when potting mix feels completely dry to the touch. Prune to keep compact. (See photo at left.)

B. m. koreana. Korean boxwood. Slower growing and smaller than Japanese boxwood.

CACTUS. Large family of succulent plants (see Succulents, page 93). Generally leafless, with stems modified into cylinders, pads, or joints that store water in times of drought. Their thick skin reduces evaporation, and most species have spines to protect plants against browsing animals. Flowers are usually large and brightly colored; fruits may be colorful, a few are edible. All (with one doubtful exception) are native to the Americas. Many are native to drier parts of the West: these like fast-draining potting mix, at least 4 hours of sun daily, watering when the soil dries out completely, fertilizing in spring and summer, and a dormant period during winter (give less water, no fertilizer). Some are jungle cactus that grow as epiphytes in trees (like some orchids): these need rich potting mix with good drainage, frequent watering and fertilizing, filtered light. For cactus that can be used as house plants, see: *Astrophytum, Cephalocereus, Chamaecereus silvestri, Echinocactus, grusonii, Echinocereus, Echinopsis, Epiphyllum, Gymnocalycium, Lobivia, Mammillaria, Notocactus, Opuntia, Rebutia, Rhipsalidopsis gaertneri, Rhipsalis paradoxa, Schlumbergera.*

CALADIUM bicolor. Fancy-leafed caladium. Native to tropical America. Grows from tubers. Brightly colored, arrow-shaped, translucent leaves in red, pink, white, green, and silver, often with a variety of colors on the same leaf. Likes good filtered light, warm temperatures (at least 70° in the daytime), high humidity. Keep potting mix constantly moist during growing season. Start tubers in March. Pot in equal parts coarse sand and leaf mold, ground bark, or peat moss. Use 5-inch pot for 2½-inch tubers; 7-inch pot for 1 larger or 2 smaller tubers. Fill pot half full with mix; stir in 1 heaping teaspoon of fish meal. Add 1 inch mix; set tuber in with knobby side up; cover with 2 inches mix. Water thoroughly. Keep soil constantly moist as leaves develop. Mist frequently. Feed with liquid fish fertilizer once a week, starting when leaves appear. Gradually withhold water when leaves start to die down. In about a month, lift tubers, remove most of soil, dry for 10 days. Store for winter in peat moss or vermiculite at temperatures between 50°-60°. (See photo, page 44.)

CALATHEA. Striking foliage plant native to tropical America, Africa. Usually called *Maranta* (see page 70), to which they are closely related. Foliage beautifully marked in shades of green, white, and pink. Requires high humidity, filtered sun (good light necessary for rich leaf color), standard potting mix, warm temperatures (above 55°). Mist frequently. Keep potting mix constantly moist but never soggy; stagnant conditions are harmful. Repot as often as necessary to avoid root bound condition. (See photos at right.)

   C. insignis. Rattlesnake plant. Long (12-18 inches), yellow green leaves striped olive green.

   C. makoyana. Peacock plant. Leaves with areas of olive green or cream above, pink blotches below.

   C. ornata. Sturdy. Leaves rich green above, purplish red below. Juvenile leaves usually pink-striped between veins.

   C. zebrina. Zebra plant. Compact growth. Long velvety green with alternating bars of pale yellow-green and olive green extending outward from midrib; purplish red underneath.

CALICO HEARTS. See Adromischus.

CALLISIA elegans. Striped inch plant. Native to Mexico. A creeper with white or yellow-striped green leaves with purple underneath. Related to *Tradescantia* (page 94) and *Zebrina* (page 95). Good for hanging containers. Grows best in filtered light, average house temperatures, standard potting mix.

Calathea insignis

Calathea makoyana

Camellia

Capsicum annuum

Check moisture level frequently (even daily); *Callisia* likes lots of water. Frequent pinching will promote compact growth.

CAMELLIA. Indoor-outdoor plant. Evergreen shrub with glossy, dark green foliage and lovely flowers in whites, pinks, reds. Blooms winter, spring. Move camellias in containers indoors to enjoy blooms for short periods of time. Indoors, likes cool temperatures, good filtered sunlight, high humidity. Plant in acid potting mix; keep mix moist with good drainage (plants don't like wet feet). Use acid fertilizer after bloom. (See photo at left.)

CAMPANULA isophylla. Italian bellflower, Star of Bethlehem. Indoor-outdoor plant. Perennial. Light green, heart-shaped, toothed leaves; pale blue, star-shaped flowers. Trailing hanging stems good for hanging baskets. Likes standard potting mix, good filtered light, good drainage.

CAPE PRIMROSE. See Streptocarpus.

CAPSICUM annuum. Ornamental pepper. Usually a colorful Christmas gift plant. Annual; may be grown from seed. Spring white flowers followed by colorful red fruit in fall. Likes at least 4 hours of sun daily, standard potting mix, cool temperatures, ample water. (See photo at left.)

CARISSA grandiflora. Natal plum. Native to South Africa. May be summered outdoors. Grown for leathery, rich green, 3-inch, oval leaves; white, star-shaped, fragrant flowers. Flowers followed by red edible fruit. Likes at least 4 hours of sun daily, high humidity, standard potting mix. Prune to keep compact. Keep potting mix constantly moist; less water needed during plant's winter rest.

CARRION FLOWERS. See Stapelia.

CARYOTA. Fishtail palm. Native to southeast Asia. Tender. Feather palms with finely divided leaves, leaflets flattened and split at tip like fish tails. Slow-growing. Likes bright light, standard potting mix. Keep potting mix wet but not swimming; never let pot stand in water. Cannot prune single stem. When plants outgrow your house, move them to a sheltered outdoor patio.

C. mitis. Clustered fishtail palm. Slow grower. Light green foliage. Very tender, not for beginners.

C. ochlandra. Canton fishtail palm. Hardiest of *Caryota*. Medium dark green leaves.

C. urens. Fishtail wine palm. Dark green leaves. Dies if temperature drops below 32°.

CAST-IRON PLANT. See Aspidistra elatior.

CATTLEYA. Large genus of epiphytic orchids native to tropical America. Most popular, best known orchid family; includes familiar corsage orchid. Plants have pseudobulbs bearing 1-3 thick, leathery, light green leaves; 1-4 flowers per stem. Flowers in all colors except blue and black. Requires warm temperatures (60° at night, 10° or more higher during the day), high humidity, good light with at least 4 hours sun daily (western or southern exposure) but protect from hot midday sun. Plant in osmunda fiber or fir bark. Water when potting mix feels dry and light weight about once a week. Feed plants with a commercial orchid fertilizer about once every two weeks during the growing season. (See photo at right.)

CENTURY PLANT. See Agave.

CEPHALOCEREUS. Columnar cactus with white hairs; native to Mexico. Slow growing. Requires at least 4 hours of sun daily, warm temperatures. Plant in standard potting mix. Water when potting mix is completely dry.

C. palmeri. Wooly torch. Hardy. Short, blue-green spines with tufts of white, wooly hair. Columnar but may branch.

C. polyanthus. Aztec column. Slow-growing column with fluted ribs, yellow-brown spines.

C. senilis. Old man cactus. Ribbed column; spines hidden in long, white hairs.

CEROPEGIA woodii. Rosary vine, String of hearts. Fast-growing succulent vine native to South Africa. Hanging or trailing stems grow from a tuberous base. Heart-shaped leaves in pairs on purplish stem are dark green marbled in silver. Tiny pink or purple flowers. Small tubers that form on stems inspired the nickname "rosary vine." Plant in sandy potting mix with extra humus; water when potting mix is dry to the touch. Likes average house temperatures, filtered sunlight. Occasionally, when the plant may appear to wilt, it is only resting, so hold back on water until new growth appears.

CESTRUM. Jessamine. Evergreen shrub native to tropical America. Grown for fragrance of showy, tubular flowers. Can be summered outdoors on shaded patio. Likes warm temperatures, at least 4 hours of sun daily, high humidity, generous watering and fertilizing. Plant in standard potting mix; keep mix constantly moist. Needs heavy pruning to stay compact.

C. nocturnum. Night Jessamine. Creamy white flowers in summer, white berries. Powerfully fragrant at night.

C. parqui. Willow-leafed jessamine. Willowlike leaves. Greenish yellow flowers, dark violet-brown berries. Potent perfume.

CHAMAECEREUS silvestri. Peanut cactus. Dwarf cactus native to Argentina. Cylindrical, ribbed, spiny joints that fall off easily and root just as easily. Heavy blooming in spring, summer. Bright red flowers to 3 inches long. Likes sun, warm temperatures, sandy potting mix. Let potting mix become dry between waterings.

CHAMAEDOREA. Generally slow-growing palm native to tropical America. Likes filtered light (can

Cattleya

Chamaedorea elegans

Chamaerops humilis

tolerate poor light; sun fades leaf color), average house temperatures and humidity, standard potting mix. Water occasionally; plants in good light situations will need more. (See photo, page 47.)

C. costaricana. Bamboolike clumps grow quickly to 8-10 feet if well watered and fertilized. Lacy, leathery leaves. May need a large container.

C. elegans *(Neanthe bella).* Parlor palm. Best indoor *Chamaedorea.* Tolerates low light, crowded roots. Grows slowly to 3-4 feet. Fertilize regularly. Repot every 2-3 years. Effective when planted 3 or more plants to a container.

C. erumpens. Bamboolike clumps with drooping leaves. Dwarf; to 4-5 feet. Needs shade.

C. geonomaeformis. Grows slowly to 4 feet. Broad, oblong leaves deeply split at tips in fishtail effect.

CHAMAERANTHEMUM. Foliage in different colors with veined patterns. May have small flowers. Likes standard potting mix, high humidity, filtered light, average house temperatures, evenly moist potting mix (never soggy).

C. gaudichaudii. Small creeper from Brazil. Silver-centered, dark green leaves.

C. igneum. Suedelike leaves veined red, yellow.

C. venosum. Grayish leaves mottled silver.

CHAMAEROPS humilis. Mediterranean fan palm. Indoor-outdoor plant. Hardy palm rarely exceeds 4-6 feet indoors. Clumps develop slowly from offshoots. Leaves green to bluish green, very spiny; keep out of traffic pattern. Likes at least 4 hours sun daily, standard potting mix, average house temperatures. Water heavily in summer to encourage growth. Fertilize in spring, summer. (See photo at left.)

CHENILLE PLANT. See Acalypha hispida.

CHIN CACTUS. See Gymnocalycium.

CHINESE BANYAN, WEEPING. See Ficus benjamina.

CHINESE EVERGREEN. See Aglaonema.

CHINESE GODDESS BAMBOO. See Bambusa.

CHINESE LANTERN. See Abutilon.

CHINESE LANTERN, WEEPING. See Abutilon megapotamicum.

CHLOROPHYTUM comosum. Spider plant. Evergreen plant native to tropics. Clumps of curving leaves like long, broad grass blades. Foliage green, or green variegated with white or yellow as margins or center strips. Tiny white flowers. Miniature duplicates of the mother plant, complete with roots, form at end of long, curved stem. Plantlets can be potted individually. Great display in hanging basket. Likes bright light, standard potting mix, average house temperatures and humidity. Let potting mix dry out between waterings. (See photo at left.)

CHOCOLATE SOLDIER. See Episcia cupreta.

Chlorophytum comosum

CHRISTMAS CACTUS. See Schlumbergera bridgesii.

CHRYSALIDOCARPUS lutescens *(Areca lutescens)*. Slow growing palm native to Malagasy. Can be summered outdoors on shaded patio. Smooth trunks, yellowish green leaves. Likes bright light, warm temperatures, standard potting mix. Water well during growing season; never let pot sit in water. Fertilize regularly in spring and summer. Spider mite can be a problem. Tricky to maintain.

CHRYSANTHEMUM morifolium. Florists' chrysanthemums. Popular gift plants with forced bloom in many colors. Plants grown outdoors in containers on patio can also be brought inside to enjoy while in bloom. To prolong bloom, give them bright light, cool temperatures, lots of water. When flowers fade, cut off; return plant outdoors and plant in ground. Do not allow to become potbound.

CIBOTIUM glaucum *(C. chamissoi)*. Hawaiian tree fern. Indoor-outdoor plant. Tree fern with feathery, golden green fronds. Likes indirect light, warm temperatures, high humidity. Plant in ½ standard potting mix, ½ peat moss or leaf mold. Keep potting mix moist but not too wet. Can spread with very broad leaf crowns.

CIGAR PLANT. See Cuphea ignea.

CISSUS. Evergreen vines. All climb by tendrils. Related to Virginia creeper, Boston ivy, and grape. Easy to grow. Likes average light, temperatures, humidity; standard potting mix. Water when soil dries out. Tolerant of adverse conditions. (See photos at right.)

   C. antarctica. Kangaroo treebine. Native to Australia. Medium green, shiny, toothed leaves to 2-3 ½ inches long.

   C. a. 'Minima'. Dwarf kangaroo ivy. Waxy green leaves on compact plant.

   C. discolor. Moss green, quilted leaves with red veins, silver markings. To 6 inches long. Toothed margin. More difficult to maintain than other *Cissus.*

   C. rhombifolia. Grape ivy. Native to South America. Dark green leaves in threes, sharp-toothed edges. Has bronze tones because of reddish hairs on veins underneath. Tolerates low light.

   C. striata. Miniature grape ivy.

CITRUS. Dwarf varieties indoor-outdoor plants. Glossy evergreen foliage, fragrant blossoms, colorful edible fruit. Plant in standard potting mix; soak potting mix completely. May need water daily. Likes at least 4 hours of sun daily. Fertilize with high-nitrogen (citrus) fertilizer in late winter, June, August. Some varieties to choose from: kumquat, lemon, lime, mandarin orange, orange, 'Rangpur' lime, and tangelo.

CLERODENDRUM thomsoniae. Bleeding heart, Glorybower. Large evergreen vine native to west Africa. Oval, dark green, ribbed leaves. Flowers:

Cissus antarctica

Cissus rhombifolia

Clerodendrum thomsoniae

Clivia miniata

Codiaeum varieties

white, lanternlike calyx opens to show red petals. Can be trained upright on supports or as a hanger. Prune to keep compact and for more blooms. Likes warm temperatures, bright light, some humidity, standard potting mix. Fertilize regularly during spring, summer. Keep potting mix constantly moist during growing season; less water needed in winter. (See photo at left.)

CLIFF-BRAKE. See Pellaea.

CLIVIA miniata. Kaffir lily. Evergreen perennial with tuberous roots native to South Africa. Dark green, bladelike leaves 1½ feet long. Brilliant clusters of orange, funnel-shaped flowers. Blooms from December to April. Plant in rich soil. Likes bright light (no direct sun), potting mix watered when dry to touch during active growth. Fertilize 2 or 3 times during growing season. Repot carefully every 2-3 years; *Clivia* likes crowded roots. (See photo at left.)

CLUB MOSS. See Selaginella kraussiana brownii.

COBRA LILY. See Darlingtonia californica.

COBWEB HOUSELEEK. See Sempervivum arachnoideum.

CODIAEUM. Croton. Tropical plant grown for colorful, leathery, glossy leaves that may be green, yellow, red, purple, bronze, pink, or almost any combination of these. Many leaf shapes. Plant grows to 15 inches (much taller in good environment). Likes bright light, warm temperatures, high humidity, standard potting mix, lots of water. Mist frequently to clean leaves, discourage pests. (See photo at left.)

    C. aucubaefolium. Gold dust plant. Bushy plant with bright green, glossy, spotted or blotched yellow leaves.

    C. spirale. Multicolored, corkscrew-twisted leaves in reds, dark gray green.

    C. variegatum. Glossy, lance-shaped leaves in spectacular shades of green, yellow, red, purple, bronze.

COELOGYNE. Epiphytic evergreen orchid native to eastern hemisphere. Dark green, spoon-shaped leaves. Small flowers in shades of brown, cream, beige, or green. Likes shade or filtered light, 55°-60° nighttime temperatures, regular fertilizing during growing season. Plant in osmunda fiber or fir bark. Excess water in new growth where flower cluster forms may cause buds to rot.

    C. cristata. To 24 inches. White flowers with yellow throat. Blooms winter to spring. Keep plant on dry side once growth has matured until after flowers fade.

    C. massangeana. To 48 inches. Ochre brown flowers with dark brown lip. May bloom twice a year—in spring and fall.

COFFEA arabica. Coffee tree. Glossy, dark green, oval leaves. Small, fragrant white flowers followed by red berries; each berry contains two coffee beans.

Likes filtered light, standard potting mix, average temperatures, high humidity. Keep potting mix moist but not soggy. Fertilize during growing season. Pinch to keep compact. (See photo at right.)

COFFEE TREE. See Coffea arabica.

COLEUS blumei. Coleus. Painted nettle. Brilliantly colored, velvety leaves, often ruffled or scalloped, in shades of green, chartreuse, yellow, salmon, peach, orange, red, magenta, purple, and brown. Leaves may contain one or several colors. Needs balanced light (too much sun or too much shade causes leaf colors to fade), warm temperatures, standard potting mix, regular fertilizing, ample water. Frequent pinching needed to encourage branching, control size. Remove flower buds.

COLOCASIA esculenta *(Caladium esculentum)*. Taro, Elephant's ear. Large perennial with tuberous roots. Native to tropical Asia and Polynesia. Mammoth, heart-shaped, gray-green leaves give exotic effect. Can be summered outdoors on shaded patio. Plant tubers in rich, moist soil. Needs warm temperatures, filtered light. Keep potting mix constantly moist and fertilize monthly during growing season.

COLUMNEA. Many species native to tropical America. Trailing stems good in hanging baskets. Many leaf shapes, either glossy or hairy. Brilliantly colored, tubular flowers to 3 inches long in red, orange, yellow, or combinations of these. Plant in packaged African violet potting mix to which small pebbles, sand, or perlite has been added. Likes average house temperatures (slightly cooler than African violets), high humidity, good light. Keep potting mix moist but not soggy. Fertilize regularly during growing season. (See photo at right.)

    C. microphylla. Tiny coppery leaves.

CORAL ALOE. See Aloe striata.

CORAL BEADS. See Sedum stahlii.

CORAL BERRY. See Ardisia crenata.

CORDYLINE *(Dracaena)*. Evergreen, palmlike shrubs. Long, bladelike leaves. Likes at least 4 hours sun daily, warm temperatures, high humidity (use humidity trays), standard potting mix. Keep potting mix moist during growing season; less water needed in winter. (See photo on page 52.)

    C. stricta. Dark green leaves with hint of purple. Lavender flowers. Cut canes to keep plant compact.

    C. terminalis. Ti. Plants may be started from "logs"—sections of stem imported from Hawaii. Can tolerate low light. Leaves have red, yellow, or color variegation.

CORN PLANT. See Dracaena fragrans.

COSTUS igneus. Spiral ginger. Native to tropical America. Smooth, glossy leaves arranged spirally on stems. Orange flowers. Plant can become large. Likes

Coffea arabica

Columnea microphylla

Cordyline terminalis

Crassula argentea

good light (can stand some sun), standard potting mix, high humidity, warm temperatures, more water than average.

COTYLEDON. Succulent. Many sizes. Likes warm temperatures, full sun. Plant in ½ standard potting mix, ½ sharp sand. Water when soil is dry to touch.

C. orbiculata. Opposing pairs of gray-green to white rounded leaves. Orange flowers on stem.

C. undulata. Silver crown. Broad, snowy, deeply toothed leaves. Orange flowers. Overhead watering removes the snowy powder.

CRAB CACTUS. See Schlumbergera truncata.

CRASSULA. Large family of succulents mostly native to South Africa. Thick, fleshy leaves. Don't count on flowers indoors. Plants can be summered outdoors. Likes sun, warm temperatures, potting mix consisting of ½ standard potting mix, ½ sharp sand. Will tolerate less than perfect conditions. Give water when potting mix dries out but never let plants shrink. (See photo at left.)

C. arborescens. Silver dollar. Branching plant similar to jade with gray-green, red-edged, red-dotted leaves.

C. argentea. Jade plant. Bright green, rounded leaves diffused with red. Branching, shrubby growth. Plants will stay small in small containers.

C. cooperi. Low growing with narrow green leaves dotted red.

C. cultrata. Propeller plant. Light green succulent leaves twisted in opposite directions.

C. deltoidea. Silver beads. Low growing. Fleshy, triangular leaves closely packed in 4 rows, giving plant a squarish cross section.

C. schmidtii. Pointed gray-green leaves with dark spot.

C. teres. Tightly packed column of pale green leaves.

C. tetragona. Upright plant with treelike habit, 1-2 feet tall. Leaves narrow. Used in dish gardens to suggest miniature pine trees.

CREEPING CHARLIE. See Pilea nummulariaefolia.

CREEPING FIG. See Ficus pumila.

CREEPING JENNIE. See Lysimachia nummularia.

CROSSANDRA infundibuliformis. Evergreen plant native to India. Grows to 1-1½ feet in 4-5 inch pot. Glossy, very dark green, gardenialike foliage. Showy flowers in scarlet-orange or coral-orange during summer; remove when spent. Likes strong filtered light, warm temperatures, high humidity, standard potting mix. Keep potting mix constantly moist but never soggy (roots should never dry out completely). Mist frequently.

CROTON. See Codiaeum.

CROWN OF THORNS. See Euphorbia milii.

CRYPTANTHUS zonatus. Zebra plant. Bromeliad native to Brazil. Grown for showy leaves. Low-growing rosette clusters to 18 inches wide. Leaves wavy, dark brown red, banded crosswise with green, brown, or white. Likes bright light, warm temperatures. Plant in equal parts coarse sand, ground bark or peat moss, and shredded or chopped osmunda. Water thoroughly when potting mix dries out. (See photo at right.)

CTENANTHE. Related to the *Maranta*. Grown for unusual foliage; leaves may be short-stalked along the stem or long-stalked and rising from the base. Insignificant white flowers. Likes good filtered light, moist standard potting mix, warm temperatures, high humidity, regular fertilizing. (See photo at right.)

C. 'Burle Marx'. To 15 inches. Leaves gray-green above, feathered with dark green; maroon underneath. Leaf stalks maroon.

C. compressa (*Bamburanta arnoldiana*). Bamburanta. Plants to 2-3 feet. Leathery oblong leaves, unequal sided to 15 inches long, waxy green on top, gray-green beneath.

C. oppenheimiana. Narrow, leathery leaves, dark green banded with silver above, purple beneath.

CUPHEA. Dwarf shrub native to Mexico and Guatemala. Indoor-outdoor plant. Colorful summer flowers. Likes standard potting mix, bright light, regular fertilizing, lots of water. Pinch tips for bushy growth.

C. hyssopifolia. False Heather. Long, narrow leaves. Tiny flowers in pink, purple, or white.

C. ignea. Cigar plant. Leafy, compact to 1 foot. Narrow, dark green leaves. Tubular, $\frac{3}{4}$-inch long flowers, bright red with dark ring at end, white tip, nickname "cigar plant." Blooms summer, fall.

CYCAS revoluta. Sago palm. Slow growing, usually with single trunk. In youth (2-3 feet tall), *Cycas* have airy, lacy appearance of ferns. With age (10 feet maximum height), they look more like a palm. Actually, related to conifers. Leaves divide into narrow, leathery, dark glossy green segments. Makes offsets. Likes filtered light, standard potting mix, average house temperatures. Needs a constant supply of water but hates wet feet. Fertilize during growing season, spring, summer.

CYCLAMEN persicum. Florist's Cyclamen. Gift plant from late fall to spring. Dark green leaves with silver markings. Flowers in pinks, reds, white resemble shooting stars. To prolong indoor bloom, give plants cool temperatures, bright light (no direct sun). Keep potting mix moist. After blooms are spent, let foliage die back; then plant tubers outdoors or discard plant. Second bloom from forced gift plant difficult.

CYMBALARIA muralis (*Linaria cymbalaria*). Kenilworth ivy. Perennial creeper native to Europe.

Cryptanthus species

Ctenanthe compressa

Cymbidium

Cyrtomium falcatum

Darlingtonia californica

Small, smooth, rounded leaves on trailing stems. Spring to fall flowers resemble tiny snapdragons; lilac blue marked with white and yellow. Good in hanging baskets, terrariums, if controlled. Likes cool temperatures, filtered light, high humidity, ample water. Plant in standard potting mix. Prune frequently to contain.

CYMBIDIUM. Terrestrial orchid native to high altitudes in southeast Asia. Can also be grown outdoors, brought indoors while in bloom. Long, narrow, grasslike foliage. Hybrid varieties have large flowers in white, pink, yellow, green, bronze with dark markings. Twelve or more flowers per stem. Miniature varieties have flowers about 1/4 the size. Need cool nighttime temperatures (45°-55°) in summer, fall to set flower buds. Give bright light, no direct sun. Foliage should be yellow green; dark green foliage indicates that plant has had too much shade. Plant in packaged *Cymbidium* orchid potting mix or mix 2 parts each fir bark, leafmold, and peat moss and 1 part sand. Keep potting mix constantly moist from March through October. Fertilize every 2 weeks from January through July, once a month August through December. Keep *Cymbidiums* potbound for better blooms. When dividing, keep a minimum of three healthy bulbs per pot.

CYPERUS. Indoor-outdoor plant. Perennial grown for striking form. Rushlike plant related to papyrus with an umbrella-shaped cluster of leaves on top of slender stems. Likes bright light, cool temperatures, standard potting mix, high humidity. Requires constant moisture; best to submerge roots in water. Divide when clumps become too large; save smaller outside divisions and discard older center. Fertilize regularly in spring, summer.

    C. alternifolius. Umbrella plant. Two to 4-foot stems. Leaves arranged like ribs of an umbrella give plant its nickname. Flowers in dry, greenish-brown clusters.

    C. a. 'Nanus'. Dwarf form.

    C. diffusus. Similar to umbrella plant but with broader leaves, more lush growth. To 12-18 inches.

    C. haspan. Dwarf papyrus. Stems to 18 inches. Long, thin leaves and flowers make filmy brown and green clusters. Delicate shape.

CYRTOMIUM falcatum. Holly fern. Native to Japan. Leaflets large, dark green, leathery, glossy, toothed like Christmas holly (which plant resembles). Grows to 2-3 feet. Good indoor fern; requires less humidity than most. Likes filtered light (sunless north exposure good), average house temperatures, moist standard potting mix. When repotting, do not bury root ball. (See photo at left.)

DARLINGTONIA californica. California pitcher plant, Cobra lily. Native to northern California, Oregon mountain bog areas. Leaf is yellow-green, hooded, red-veined, pitcher-shaped for capturing insects. Decayed, trapped insects become food for plant. Grows to 15 inches. Plant in live sphagnum moss; keep moist at all times. Do not use alkaline water—rainwater is the safest. Likes filtered light, cool temperatures. Children enjoy these novelty, insect-eating plants. (See photo, page 54.)

DAVALLIA. Group of ferns with brownish, furry creeping stems (rhizomes) that grow above ground. Stems give nicknames (see below) because they resemble animals' feet. All forms good in hanging baskets or on pedestals. Fronds feathery, dark green. Like filtered light (sunless north exposure best), cool temperatures, high humidity. Mist frequently or use humidity trays. Plant in ½ standard potting mix, ½ peat moss. Keep potting mix moist but don't overwater. Feed occasionally. (See photo at right.)

D. bullata mariesii. Ball fern. Smallest form; grows to 6-8 inches. Brown rhizomes.

D. fijiensis. Rabbit's foot fern. Brown, wooly, creeping rhizomes.

D. trichomanoides. Squirrel's foot fern. Large fronds to 12 inches tall. Light reddish brown rhizomes.

DEVIL'S BACKBONE. See Pedilanthus tithymaloides.

DEVIL'S IVY. See Rhaphidophora aurea.

DIEFFENBACHIA. Dumb cane, Mother-in-law plant. Evergreen foliage plant native to tropical America. Nickname "dumb cane" refers to fact that the acrid sap in leaves will burn mouth and throat and may paralyze vocal cords. Usually single stem; older plants may develop multiple stems. Grows to 6 feet or taller. Large, pointed, variegated leaves; colors vary from dark green to yellow-green and chartreuse, with variegation in white or pale cream. Likes filtered light (sunless northern exposure good), standard potting mix, average house temperatures and humidity. Water when potting mix feels dry. Fertilize regularly in spring, summer. Air layer leggy plants. (See photo at right.)

D. amoena. To 6 feet or higher. Dark green, 18-inch leaves with white, slanting stripes on either side of midrib.

D. 'Exotica.' Smaller leaves; more compact growth. Leaves dull green with creamy white variegation.

D. picta. Wide, oval green leaves with greenish white dots and patches; to 10 inches long.

D. p. 'Rudolph Roehrs'. Pale chartreuse leaves blotched with ivory, edged in green, to 10 inches long.

D. p. 'Superba'. Thick, durable foliage with more variegation than other varieties.

DIONAEA muscipula. Venus flytrap. Insect-eating plant native to the Carolinas. Does not need insects to survive. Yellow-green leaves edged with hairs, hinged at center. Grows to 6 inches. Full sun brings

Davallia trichomanoides

Dieffenbachia

Dionaea muscipula

Dizygotheca elegantissima

Dracaena fragrans 'Massangeana'

out the deep red coloring inside open leaf. Likes high humidity (especially good in terrariums), cool temperatures (around 60°), lots of water. Plant in sphagnum moss mixed with a little sand and peat moss. (See photo, page 55.)

DIPLADENIA. See Mandevilla 'Alice du Pont'.

DIZYGOTHECA elegantissima *(Aralia elegantissima).* Thread-leaf, false aralia. Lacy, evergreen leaves that are dark green, glossy above, reddish brown underneath. Leaves divided fanwise into very narrow, 4 to 9-inch-long leaflets with notched edges. Likes bright light (no direct sun), standard potting mix with good drainage, high humidity, average house temperatures. Improper watering may cause problems; dry or waterlogged soil causes leaf drop. Fertilize regularly. (See photo at left.)

DONKEY TAIL. See Sedum morganianum.

DRACAENA (Cordyline). Evergreen palmlike plants. Long, bladelike foliage, either green or variegated. Can become tall. Likes bright light, standard potting mix, average house temperatures and humidity, regular fertilizing and watering. Will tolerate abuse—low light, low humidity, infrequent watering. Plants effective when planted 3 to a pot. (See photo at left.)

    D. deremensis 'Warneckii'. Leaves 2 feet long, 2 inches wide; rich green with white and gray streaks running lengthwise.

    D. draco. Dragon tree. Slow growing with unusual form. Heavy, sword-shaped leaves.

    D. fragrans. Corn plant. Green, cornlike leaves.

    D. fragrans 'Massangeana'. Green, cornlike leaves with broad yellow stripe in center of leaf.

    D. godseffiana. Gold dust plant. Small, slow grower. Dark green leaves irregularly spotted with yellow or white.

    D. marginata. Blade-shaped, deep olive green leaves edged with red. Needs bright light to maintain color.

    D. sanderiana. Ribbon plant. Upright growing. Resembles a young corn plant. Green with white stripes. Good for dish gardens, terrariums.

DRAGON TREE. See Dracaena draco.

DUMB CANE. See Dieffenbachia.

DYCKIA fosteriana. Bromeliad native to tropical America. Leaves of silvery gray, occasionally reddish brown, in rosette form with spike-toothed edges, sharp tips. Orange flowers on tall slender stems. Likes full sun (don't let foliage burn), average house temperatures and humidity, regular fertilizing. Plant in equal parts standard potting mix, sand, and peat moss or fir bark. Let potting mix dry out between waterings. (See photo, page 57.)

EASTER CACTUS. See Rhipsalidopsis gaertneri.

EASTER LILY CACTUS. See Echinopsis.

ECHEVERIA. Succulent native to the Americas. Rosette form with fleshy leaves of green or gray-green, sometimes marked with deeper colors. Flowers form in clusters on long stems, are bell-shaped in pink, red, yellow. Likes full sun, warm temperatures. Plant in equal parts sharp sand, standard potting mix. Water when potting mix is completely dry to touch.

E. derenbergii. Painted lady. Small, tight, spreading rosettes. Leaves grayish white with red edges. Reddish and yellow flowers.

E. elegans. Mexican snowball. Silver blue rosette frosted white. Pink flowers.

E. glauca. Hen and chicks. Purple-tinted, gray green rosettes.

E. imbricata. Hen and chicks. Gray green rosettes.

E. pulvinata. Round hairy leaves covered with silvery down that later turns red. Red flowers.

ECHINOCACTUS grusonii. Golden barrel. Cactus with cylindrical shape native to Mexico. Slow growing. Straight, sharp, yellow spines; with age, develops crown of yellow wool. Yellow flowers. Likes sun, warm temperatures. Plant in equal parts standard potting mix, sharp sand. Let potting mix completely dry out between waterings; in winter, give only enough to keep plant from shrinking.

ECHINOCEREUS. Desert cactus requiring little attention. Usually less than 12 inches tall. Ornamental spines. Showy flowers. Likes warm temperatures, full sun. Plant in equal parts standard potting mix, sharp sand, occasional water.

E. baileyi. Columnar growth, white spines. Yellow flowers.

E. dasyacanthus. Rainbow cactus. Small, columnar plant covered with soft spines. Large yellow flowers.

E. ehrenbergii. Stem erect, free-branching from base; glassy white spines. Purple-red flowers.

E. reichenbachii. Lace cactus. Small, heavily spined. Red and yellow flowers.

ECHINOPSIS. Easter lily cactus, Sea urchin cactus. Small cylindrical or globular cactus native to South America. Large showy flowers in white, yellow, pink, red. Free blooming in summer if given good light, frequent fertilizing. Likes at least 4 hours of sun daily, warm temperatures. Plant in equal parts standard potting mix, sharp sand. Water when soil dries.

ELATIOR BEGONIAS. See Begonia.

ELEPHANT'S EAR. See Colocasia esculenta.

EMERALD RIPPLE. See Peperomia caprata 'Emerald Ripple'.

EPIDENDRUM. Easy-to-grow orchids native to tropical America, epiphytic or terrestrial. Variable in flower and plant form. Some have pseudobulbs and require a rest after flowering; others are cane-stemmed and need moisture all year. Flowers in many

Dyckia fosteriana

Epidendrum ibaguense

Epiphyllum

Episcia cupreata

Euonymus japonica 'Microphylla'

colors. Plant in ground fir bark, osmunda fiber, or packaged orchid potting mix. Most like sun, warm temperatures, and high humidity. Fertilize regularly.

E. atropurpureum. To 16 inches with pseudobulbs. Three-inch, chocolate brown and pale green flowers with white and purple markings; 4-20 flowers per stem. Bloom spring, early summer. Rest plants after blooming.

E. ibaguense (*E. radicans*). Native to Colombia. To 2-4 feet with reedlike, leafy stems. Dense flower clusters. Orange-yellow flowers with fringed lip. Numerous hybrids with flowers in yellow, orange, pink, red, lavender, white; generally sold by color.

E. nemorale. To 16 inches. Large, 4-inch, rose and purple flowers. Blooms spring, summer.

E. stamfordianum. To 30 inches with tiny, yellow and red flowers. Pseudobulb. Blooms spring.

EPIPHYLLUM. Orchid cactus. Epiphytic jungle cactus. Can be summered outdoors on shaded patio. Spineless, has flattened stems with scalloped edges. Large, showy flowers in many colors that bloom April to June. Plant in sandy soil with good drainage. Keep plant potbound for best results. Likes bright light, cool nighttime temperatures (50°), high humidity. Let potting mix dry out thoroughly between waterings. Rest plants in winter. Natural growth is pendent; stake plants for upright growth. (See photo at left.)

EPISCIA. Peacock plant, Flame violet. Oval, 4-inch, velvety-hairy foliage colored from green to brown with metallic sheen in silver, bronze, green; frequently veined or mottled in contrasting colors. Leaf type similar to African violets. *Episcia* produces runners like strawberries, with plantlets forming at runner ends; growth ideal for hanging baskets. Tubular flowers usually red-orange, but hybrid plant colors include pink, yellow, white, lavender, combinations. Likes warm temperatures (60° or higher at night; 75° during day), high humidity, bright light (no direct sun), regular fertilizing, lots of water (more than for African violets). Plant in packaged African violet potting mix. (See photo at left.)

E. cupreata. Oval coppery leaves. Orange-red flowers. Variety 'Metallica' has olive-green leaves with pale stripes, red margins. 'Chocolate Soldier' has chocolate brown, silver-veined leaves.

E. dianthiflora. Small-leafed variety. Leaves all green. White flowers.

E. lilacina. Dark, bronze green leaves, sometimes patterned green. Pale lavender flowers with yellow throat.

E. punctata. Gray-green leaves. Fringed creamy-white flowers spotted purple. Good bloomer.

E. reptans (**E. fulgens**). Pebbled bronze leaves with willow green veins. Red flowers.

EUONYMUS japonica 'Microphylla'. Box-leaf Euonymus. Compact, small-leafed evergreen shrub.

Grown for foliage. Good in dish gardens, terrariums. Likes standard potting mix, filtered light, cool temperatures (can tolerate from 35°-75°), regular watering. Prune frequently to keep compact. 'Microphylla Variegata' has leaves splashed white. Yellow variegation on 'Golden Queen'. 'Silver Queen' has creamy white edges. (See photo, page 58.)

EUPHORBIA. Spurge. Large group of plants, many succulents. Most have acrid, milky sap (poisonous in some species) that can irritate skin. "Flower" is really colored bracts; true flowers are centered in bracts. Give strong, filtered light, warm, even temperatures. Plant in equal parts standard potting mix, sharp sand. Watering differs among species. Fertilize during growing seasons. (See photo at right.)

E. hermentiana *(E. trigona)*. Slow growing. Interesting silhouette. Three-angled, toothed stems with fleshy wings at each angle. Small, oblong leaves. Can tolerate drought but prefers regular watering.

E. lactea 'Cristata'. Dwarf, crested, bizarre form resembles *E. hermentiana* with same water needs. Broad, green and gray, coralloid mass to 12 inches.

E. milii. Crown of thorns. Succulent, woody perennial native to Malagasy. Legend says flowers were once white but turned red when stems were used to make the crown of thorns Jesus wore. Tall stems to 3-4 feet, long sharp thorns. Leaves roundish, thin, light green, found only near branch ends. Red bracts (yellow, orange, pink varieties also). Needs bright light, no direct sun. May bloom all year. Can tolerate drought but prefers regular watering.

E. obesa. Baseball plant. Succulent. Fleshy, gray-green cylinder to 8 inches tall with brownish striplings, brown dots that resemble stitching on a baseball. Keep dryish in winter.

E. 'Pink Sensation'. Hummel hybrid, known as giant crown of thorns or Christ thorn hybrids. Larger stems, leaves, and flowers than *E. milii*. Six to eight flowers at stalk ends. Blooms continually. Likes regular watering.

E. pulcherrima. Poinsettia. Usually a blooming Christmas gift plant. Bracts in red (most common), pink, white. To prolong bloom, keep in sunny window with constant temperatures. Keep potting mix moist. After blooming, cut stems back to 2 buds, reduce water, keep in cool spot, and then set outside (when all danger of frost is past) in sun. Difficult to repeat blooming indoors.

FALSE SEA ONION. See Ornithogalum caudatum.

FATSHEDERA lizei. Vine that climbs like ivy. Hybrid between *Fatsia japonica* and *Hedera helix*. Highly polished leaves with 3-5 pointed lobes, 6-8 inches wide. Likes bright light (protect from hot sun), average house temperatures and humidity, standard potting mix, ample water. Prune to keep compact. Needs support to climb. (See photo at right.)

F. l. 'Variegata'. White bordered leaves.

From left: Euphorbia 'Pink Sensation', *E. hermentiana, E. lactea* 'Cristata'

Fatshedera lizei

Ficus diversifolia

Ficus elastica

FATSIA japonica *(Aralia sieboldii, A. japonica)*. Japanese aralia. Tropical evergreen shrub with glossy, dark green, deeply-lobed, fanlike leaves. Small, whitish flowers fall, winter; remove flower buds for better foliage. Use young plants indoors; prune or pinch to keep compact. Likes bright light, cool temperatures (not over 70°), standard potting mix, regular waterings.

F. j. 'Moseri'. Compact, low growing.

F. j. 'Variegata'. Leaves edged golden yellow to creamy white.

FELT PLANT. See Kalanchoe beharensis.

FERN. Large group of perennial plants grown for foliage. Leaves are usually finely cut. No flowers. They reproduce by spores that form directly on the fronds. Although most are native to forests, some grow in deserts, in open fields, or near timberline in high mountains. Tree ferns may grow to 50 feet or more. Native ferns are smaller, with handsome fronds. Most like rich potting mix, filtered light, and lots of moisture. All ferns look best if groomed; remove dead or injured fronds by cutting off near the soil surface. Fertilize during growing season. For ferns that will grow indoors, see: *Asplenium, Cibotium glaucum, Cyrtomium falcatum, Davallia, Humata tyermannii, Nephrolepis, Phyllitis scolopedrium, Platycerium, Polystichum, Pteris.*

FICUS. Ornamental fig. Diverse family of trees, shrubs, vines. Ornamental foliage. Likes standard potting mix, bright light (no direct sun), regular fertilizing. Let soil dry out between waterings. (See photos at left, and on page 61.)

F. benjamina. Weeping Chinese banyan, Weeping fig. Evergreen. Shiny green leathery leaves, 2-5 inches long. New growth pale green, older leaves dark green. Drooping branches, delicate appearance.

F. diversifolia. Mistletoe fig. Evergreen. Native to Malaysia. Slow growing. Open, twisted branch pattern. Two-inch leaves are round, thick, dark green with tan specks on upper surface, black specks below. Small yellow fruits. Prune to maintain preferred size. Needs more water than other *Ficus.*

F. elastica. Rubber plant. Native to India, Malaysia. Very easy house plant. Leaves thick, glossy, leathery, dark green, 8-12 inches long by 4-6 inches wide. Can tolerate drought.

F. e 'Decora' *(F. e.* 'Belgica'). Broader, glossier leaves than *F. elastica,* bronze when young.

F. e. 'Rubra'. New leaves reddish; red edge maintained as rest of leaf turns green.

F. e. 'Variegata' *(F. doescheri).* Long, narrow leaves are variegated yellow and green.

F. lyrata *(F. pandurata).* Fiddleleaf fig. Native to tropical Africa. Large, dark green, glossy leaves, fiddle-shaped to 15 inches long, 10 inches wide. Prune top to make plant bushy. Tolerates low light. Doesn't require a large pot. Keep leaves clean.

F. pumila *(F. repens).* Creeping fig. Evergreen vine native to China, Japan, Australia. Tiny, heart-shaped, delicate leaves. Difficult to grow indoors.

F. retusa nitida. Similar to *F. benjamina* but with straighter branches and fewer leaves. Needs frequent pruning for shape.

FIDDLELEAF FIG. See Ficus lyrata.

FIG, ORNAMENTAL. See Ficus.

FIG, WEEPING. See Ficus.

FINGERNAIL PLANT. See Neoregelia spectabilis.

FIRE CROWN. See Rebutia senilis.

FITTONIA verschaffeltii. Nerve plant, Mosaic plant. Evergreen creeper native to South America. Dark green, oval leaves veined with red or bright pink. Likes indirect light (north exposure good), high humidity, warm temperatures, regular fertilizing, standard potting mix, lots of water (never let potting mix dry out completely). (See photo, page 62.)

F. v. 'Argyroneura'. Leaves veined white.

FLAME VIOLET. See Episcia.

FLAMINGO FLOWER. See Anthurium scherzerianum.

FLUFFY RUFFLES. See Nephrolepis exaltata 'Fluffy Ruffles'.

FOXTAIL ASPARAGUS. See Asparagus densi-florus 'Myeri'.

FRECKLE FACE. See Hypoestes sanguinolenta.

FREESIA. Corm. Native to South Africa. Stems to 1-1½ feet tall. Lower leaves large, stem leaves shorter. Two-inch, tubular flowers are fragrant in white, yellow, pink, red, lavender, purple, blue, orange; spring bloom. Plant corms 2 inches deep, 2 inches apart in pots. Likes sun, cool nighttime temperatures, standard potting mix. Easily grown from seed sown in July-August; may bloom following spring.

FUCHSIA. Lady's eardrop. Indoor-outdoor plant. Upright or trailing stems. Trailing varieties good in hanging baskets. Bring indoors to enjoy bloom, or to protect from winter frost. Beautiful flowers in many color combinations and sizes. Likes filtered light (or a shaded patio), cool temperatures, frequent fertilizing, standard potting mix with excellent drainage, high humidity. Keep potting mix constantly moist. Water daily.

GARDENIA jasminoides. Indoor-outdoor plant. Evergreen shrub native to China. Shiny, bright green leaves. White, very fragrant flowers. Needs warm days with bright light, cool nighttime temperatures, regular fertilizing, lots of water (more than most indoor plants). Plant in equal parts standard potting mix and peat moss or ground bark. Keep potting mix constantly moist.

Ficus elastica 'Variegata'

Ficus lyrata

Ficus retusa nitida

Fittonia verschaffeltii 'Argyroneura'

Guzmania lingulata

GASTERIA. Oxtongue. Succulent native to South America. Long, flat leaves. Likes full sun (tolerates less), average house temperatures. Plant in equal parts standard potting mix, sharp sand. Water when potting mix is completely dry to touch.

G. liliputana. Mottled dark green, pale green leaves arranged spirally.

G. verrucosa. Tapered pink, purple leaves with white, wartlike lumps.

GEOGENANTHUS undatus. Seersucker plant. Tropical plant native to Peru. Silvery-green striped leaves with rich purple underneath; "seersucker'" texture. Grows to 1 foot; prune to keep compact. Likes warm temperatures, filtered light, high humidity, standard potting mix. Keep potting mix moist.

GERANIUM. See Pelargonium.

GLORYBOWER. See Clerodendrum thomsoniae.

GLOXINIA. See Sinningia speciosa.

GOAT'S HORN. See Astrophytum capricorne.

GOLD DUST PLANT. See Aucuba japonica 'Variegata', Codiaeum aucubaefolium, Dracaena godseffiana.

GOLDEN BAMBOO. See Phyllostachys aurea.

GOLDEN BARREL. See Echinocactus grusonii.

GOLDFISH PLANT. See Hypocyrta nummularia.

GRAPE, EVERGREEN. See Rhoicissus.

GRAPE IVY. See Cissus rhombifolia.

GREVILLEA robusta. Silk oak. Fast-growing tree native to Australia. Use immature plant indoors; move outside when tree becomes too big. Graceful, showy, golden green to deep green leaves with silvery cast. May require support to stay upright. Needs filtered light, standard potting mix, temperatures from 50°-65°. Likes ample water, good drainage. Prune frequently to keep compact.

GUZMANIA lingulata. Bromeliad native to tropical America. Rosette of smooth, metallic green leaves centered with red bracts; inner bracts are orange red, tipped white or yellow. Inconspicuous white flowers. Likes diffused light (direct sun may burn leaves), warm temperatures, high humidity, regular fertilizing. Plant in fast-draining, moisture-retentive potting mix. Give ample moisture and keep "vase" filled with water. (See photo at left.)

GYMNOCALYCIUM. Chin cactus. Cactus with globular bodies, regularly arranged protrusions that give nickname. Flowers are red, pink, white. Likes sun, average indoor temperatures. Plant in equal parts standard potting mix and sharp sand. Water when potting mix dries out; during winter rest give only enough water to keep plant from shriveling.

G. mihanovichii. Gray-green globe. Blooms at early age.

GYNURA aurantiaca. Velvet plant. Tropical plant native to East Indies. Dark green, lance-shaped, toothed leaves covered with purple hairs, giving foliage a velvety appearance. Needs strong light for best leaf color, standard potting mix, average temperatures, regular fertilizing. Likes lots of water; mist foliage frequently for humidity. Flowers have unpleasant smell; snap off all buds. Prune to keep compact.

HAEMARIA discolor. Jewel orchid. Orchid grown for foliage instead of flowers. Striking dark green, velvety foliage with red pinstriping. Needs bright light, warm temperatures, rich potting mix with good drainage, high humidity (good in large terrariums). Don't disturb roots; plant has rhizomatic growth. Plant in large, shallow container. Fertilize during growing season. (See photo at right.)

HARE'S FOOT FERN. See Polypodium aureum.

HART'S TONGUE FERN. See Phyllitis scolopedrium.

HAWORTHIA. Succulents of the lily family native to South Africa. Variable in growth habit. Best-known ones resemble small aloes; others make small towers of neatly stacked fleshy leaves. Likes shade or sunless north exposure, average temperatures. Plant in equal parts standard potting mix and sharp sand. Let potting mix dry out between waterings.

H. fasciata. Zebra haworthia. Zebra-striped rosette. Leaves dark green; raised white dots.

H. setata. Lace haworthia. Small rosette with many leaves. Dark green leaves marked with white translucent areas edged with bristly white teeth.

HEATHER, FALSE. See Cuphea hyssopifolia.

HEDERA helix. English ivy. Evergreen vine. Dark, dull green leaves with paler vines. Many types of growth habits. Needs constant temperatures (very little fluctuation), standard potting mix. Tolerant of low light situations. Let potting mix dry out *slightly* between waterings. Soil should feel slightly damp and spongy. Fertilize every two months. Mist frequently to discourage mites. Prune to keep desired size and shape. A sampling of varieties is listed below. (See photos at right, and on page 64.)

H. h. 'Baltica'. Small dark green leaves with five deeply cut lobes.

H. h. 'Californian'. Bushy with five-lobed medium green leaves that are wavy at apex. Hard to find.

H. h. 'Fan'. Develops long vines. Five to seven-lobed, dark green leaves, wavy at notches. Hard to find.

H. h. 'Glacier'. Variegated form. Triangular, leathery, dark green leaves bordered white. Needs more light than other varieties.

H. h. 'Hibernica'. Irish ivy. Largest of the varieties. Dense growth. Five-inch, round, deep green leaves with lighter green veining.

Haemaria discolor

Hedera helix

Hedera helix 'Fan'

Hibiscus rosa-sinensis

H. h. 'Marginata'. Variegated form with leathery leaves; leaves have three to five lobes green marked gray and edged white. Edges will sometimes turn reddish. Needs more light than other varieties.

H. h. 'Needlepoint'. Sharply pointed, dark green leaves.

H. h. 'Star'. Self-branching and bushy. Five-pointed, star-shaped leaves. Hard to find.

H. h. 'Sweetheart'. Heart-shaped, dark green leaves with no visible lobes.

HEDYSCEPE canterburyana. Palm native to Lord Howe Island in the South Pacific. Related to *Howeia* but smaller, broader, lower growing with broader leaf segments and more arching, lighter green, feather-type leaves. Likes filtered light, warm temperatures around 75°, standard potting mix. Give ample water. Fertilize during growing season.

HEIMERLIODENDRON brunonianum 'Variegatum'. Pisonia. A native of New Zealand. this plant grows slowly to 4 to 6 feet indoors. Variegated leaves with markings in varying shades of green with ivory border. Likes warm constant temperatures, standard potting mix, some sun to retain mottling. Feed and water regularly. (See photo, back cover.)

HELXINE. See Soleirolia soleirolii.

HEN AND CHICKENS. See Sempervivum tectorum.

HEN AND CHICKS. See Echeveria glauca, E. imbricata.

HIBISCUS rosa-sinensis. Chinese hibiscus, Tropical hibiscus. Indoor-outdoor plant. Evergreen shrub with glossy foliage; varies in size and texture. Compact varieties best in containers. Flowers 4-8 inches wide, single or double, in white, pink, red, yellow, orange, apricot. Bring indoors when frost threatens during late fall through spring. Will bloom indoors if temperatures constant at 60°-70°. Retains foliage to 40°. Likes sun, standard potting mix with excellent drainage, regular fertilizing twice a month. Water frequently. Pruning needed to keep compact. Prune tops and, if needed, roots in fall when plant moves indoors. Return to partially shaded patio when frost danger gone, late April, May. Some compact varieties: 'Bride,' 'California Gold,' 'Flamingo Plume,' 'Florida Sunset,' 'Red Dragon,' 'White Wings Compacta.' (See photo at left.)

HIPPEASTRUM. Amaryllis. Bulb native to tropics, subtropics. Broad, strap-shaped leaves appear after flowers. Two to several huge (8-9 inches across) flowers form on long, thick stem. Available colors include red, pink, white, salmon, near orange; some mottled or striped. Spring blooming. Plant bulbs November-February in rich, sandy soil mix with added bonemeal. Allow 2-inch space between bulb and pot edge. Set upper half of bulb above soil surface; firm soil and water well. Keep potting mix just barely moist until growth starts. Likes warm temperatures, sun, some humidity, regular fertilizing every two weeks through flowering stage. When flowers fade, cut off stem. Continue watering to encourage leaf growth. When leaves turn yellow, withhold water, let plants dry out. Repot in late fall, early winter.

HOLLY, FALSE. See Osmanthus heterophyllus.

HOLLY, MINIATURE. See Malpighia coccigua.

HOLLY FERN. See Cyrtomium falcatum.

HOWEIA. Kentia palm. Palm native to Lord Howe Island in South Pacific. Slow growing. Feathery leaves drop to expose clean, green trunk ringed with leaf scars. Likes warm temperatures, standard potting mix, ample moisture. Fertilize during growing season. Tolerant of low light, some watering neglect.

H. belmoreana. Sentry palm. Arching leaves. More compact than *H. forsteriana.*

H. forsteriana. Paradise palm. Leaves to 9 feet (less indoors) with long, drooping leaflets.

HOUSELEEK. See Sempervivum.

HOYA. Wax flower, Wax plant. Shrubby or climbing house plant. May need support to climb. Thick, waxy leaves. Tight clusters of small, waxy flowers. Likes sun, some humidity, constant temperatures 70°, standard potting mix. Let soil go partially dry between waterings. Plant goes semi-dormant in winter, requiring less light, less water (let potting mix go almost completely dry), lower temperatures. Keep plants potbound for best bloom. Fertilize every 2 months during growing season. Do not prune out flowering wood; new blossom clusters appear from stumps of old ones. (See photos at right.)

H. bella. Shrubby. Older branches droop; good for hanging baskets. Small leaves. Tight clusters of white, purple-centered, summer flowers.

H. carnosa. Long, oval leaves. Immature leaves red. Big, round, tight clusters of creamy white flowers; each flower has 5-pointed pink star in center. Summer blooming, fragrant.

H. c. 'Compacta'. Crinkly, closely spaced leaves.

H. c. 'Variegata'. Leaves edged in white suffused with pink.

HUMATA tyermannii. Bear's foot fern. Small fern native to China. Furry creeping rhizomes resemble bear's feet. Fronds 8-10 inches long, very finely cut. Like *Davallia* in appearance but slower growing. Likes filtered light (sunless north exposure good), cool indoor temperatures, high humidity. Plant in equal parts standard potting mix and peat moss. Likes lots of water.

HYACINTHUS. Hyacinth. Bulb. Narrow, bright green leaves. Bell-shaped, fragrant, spring-blooming flowers in shades of white, cream, pink, red, purple,

Hoya carnosa

Hoya bella

Hypocyrta nummularia

Hypoestes sanguinolenta

blue. Pot in porous mix with tip of bulb near surface. Keep bulbs cool, moist, shaded until tops show growth; then move into light. Also grow in water in special hyacinth glass. Keep in dark, cool spot until rooted. When top growth appears, place in sunny window.

HYDRANGEA macrophylla. Deciduous shrub. Indoor-outdoor plant. Popular blooming gift plant. Bold, thick, coarsely toothed leaves. Large flower cluster in white, pink, red, blue. To prolong bloom indoors, keep in filtered light with some humidity, cool temperatures (not over 70°). Keep potting mix constantly moist; *hydrangea* is a real water lover. After blooming, place plant outdoors in ground or keep in container. Keep well watered; feed regularly.

HYPOCYRTA nummularia. Goldfish plant. Pairs of shiny, thick, dark green, succulent leaves on arching branches. Good in hanging baskets. Inch-long, fat, orange flowers with pinched mouths; blooms resemble goldfish. Likes warm temperatures, high humidity, bright light (can take some morning sun), regular fertilizing. Plant in packaged African violet potting mix; give enough water at room temperature to keep mix moist. (See photo at left.)

HYPOESTES sanguinolenta. Freckle face, Pink polka-dot plant. Foliage plant native to Malagasy. Long, oval, medium green leaves irregularly spotted with pink. Variety 'Splash' has larger spots. Likes filtered light, warm temperatures, some humidity, regular fertilizing. Plant in equal parts standard potting mix and peat moss; keep moisture level constant. Pinch tips to keep bushy. (See photo at left.)

IMPATIENS walleriana. Balsam, Busy Lizzie, Patient Lucy, Touch-me-not. Perennial, usually grown as an annual. Use dwarf or semi-dwarf varieties indoors. You can summer plants outdoors on shaded patio. For best effect, plant several to a container. Dark green, glossy, narrow leaves. Flowers in scarlet, pink, rose, violet, orange, white. Likes filtered light or sunless north exposure, standard potting mix kept moist, high humidity, cool to average house temperatures.

INCH PLANT, STRIPED. See Callisia elegans.

INDIAN HEAD. See Notocactus ottonis.

IRESINE herbstii. Blood-leaf. Foliage plant native to Brazil. Translucent, crimson or yellowish, oval leaves. Color may vary. Likes bright light (needed for best leaf color), average house temperatures and humidity, standard potting mix. Let potting mix dry out between waterings. Fertilize regularly. Needs pruning to stay compact. (See photo page 67.)

IRON CROSS BEGONIA. See Begonia masoniana.

IVY. See Hedera.

IVY, ENGLISH. See Hedera.

IVY, GERMAN. See Senecio.

IVY, GRAPE. See Cissus.

IVY, KENILWORTH. See Cymbalaria.

IVY GERANIUM. See Pelargonium peltatum.

JADE PLANT. See Crassula argentea.

JAPANESE ARALIA. See Fatsia japonica.

JAPANESE AUCUBA. See Aucuba japonica.

JAPANESE BOXWOOD. See Buxus microphylla japonica.

JAPANESE PRIVET. See Ligustrum japonicum 'Texanum'.

JAPANESE SWEET FLAG. See Acorus.

JERUSALEM CHERRY. See Solanum pseudo-capsicum.

JASMINE, MADAGASCAR. See Stephanotis floribunda.

JESSAMINE. See Cestrum.

JEWEL ORCHID. See Haemaria discolor.

KAFFIR LILY. See Clivia miniata.

KALANCHOE. Succulents native to Malagasy. Shapes and sizes vary. Flowers fairly large, bell-shaped. Likes sun or bright light, warm temperatures. Plant in equal parts standard potting mix and sharp sand. Water when potting mix dries out. After blooming, prune tops and hold watering until new growth starts. (See photos at right, and on page 68.)

K. beharensis (Kitchingia mandrakensis). Felt plant. Larger than most Kalanchoes. Leaves at stem tips; each leaf 4-8 inches long, half as wide, triangular to lance-shaped, thick, and heavily covered with dense white to brown feltlike hairs. Foliage waved and crimped at edges. Hybrids differ in leaf size, color, degree of felting.

K. blossfeldiana. Popular Christmas gift plant. Fleshy, shiny leaves, dark green edged red, either smooth-edged or scalloped. Small, bright red flowers in clusters. Other varieties in yellow, orange, salmon. Blooms winter, spring.

K. daigremontiana. Maternity plant. Single-stemmed. Fleshy leaves 6-8 inches long, $1\frac{1}{4}$ or more inches wide, gray-green spotted in red. Leaf edges notched; new plantlets sprout in notches, giving nickname. Small, grayish-purple flower clusters.

K. flammea. Lightly branched. Twelve to sixteen inches tall with fleshy, gray-green, $2\frac{1}{2}$ inch leaves. Flower clusters in orange-red, yellow. Winter, spring bloom.

K. pinnata (Bryophyllum pinnatum). Air plant. Fleshy leaves; immature ones scalloped, older ones divided into 3-5 leaflets, also scalloped. Produces plantlets at the notches of the scallops. Flowers greenish white to reddish. Tolerant of low light. Likes moisture.

Iresine herbstii

Kalanchoe beharensis

Kalanchoe blossfeldiana

Kalanchoe tomentosa

Kohleria amabilis

K. tomentosa. Panda plant. Leaves very fleshy, 2 inches long, coated with dense white hairs. Leaf tips and notches in leaves marked dark brown.

KANGAROO IVY, DWARF. See Cissus antarctica 'Minima'.

KANGAROO TREEBINE. See Cissus antarctica.

KENTIA PALM. See Howeia.

KOHLERIA. Native to tropical America. Can be staked for upright growth or let hang. Rhizomatic. Fuzzy, plain green or patterned leaves. Velvety-hairy tubular flowers with flat, 5-lobed faces in reds, pinks, whites. Some have purple dots contrasting with flower color. Likes average house temperatures, filtered light, high humidity, regular fertilizing. Plant in packaged African violet potting mix kept constantly moist. Remove all old growth for continued bloom and plant health. (See photo at left.)

K. amabilis. Good in hanging baskets. Leaves soft green patterned with purplish green. Flowers bright pink with darker streaks.

K. bogotensis. Dark green foliage marked in pale green or white; brownish red underneath. Flowers bright red, yellow dots.

K. eriantha. Red leaf margins. Flowers orange red with yellow markings on lower 3 lobes.

K. lindeniana. Leaves veined silver with bronze margins. Compact growth. Flowers white with violet markings.

KOREAN BOXWOOD. See Buxus microphylla koreana.

LACE CACTUS. See Echinocereus reichenbachii.

LACE HAWORTHIA. See Haworthia setata.

LADY-OF-THE-NIGHT. See Brassavola nodosa.

LADY PALM. See Rhapis.

LADY WASHINGTON PELARGONIUM. See Pelargonium domesticum.

LADY'S SLIPPER. See Paphiopedilum.

LAELIA. Epiphytic orchid mostly native to Mexico. *Cattleya*-type foliage and flowers. One or two evergreen bladelike leaves atop pseudobulbs. Flowers smaller than *Cattleyas* with narrower petals. Need at least four hours sun (south or west exposure; sun needed for best flowering), warm temperatures (60° at night, at least 10° or more higher during the day), high humidity. Plant in osmunda fiber or fir bark. Let potting mix dry out between waterings. After flowering and until new growth starts, *Laelias* need very little water. Feed plants about every two weeks with an orchid fertilizer during growing season. (See photo page 69.)

L. gouldiana. To 30 inches. Three-inch, deep rose flowers in winter.

L. pumila. To 10 inches. Rose-purple flowers with yellow-throated purple lips in fall.

L. superbiens. To 5 feet when in bloom. Six-inch, lavender, purple-throated blooms in clusters of 10-20 flowers per stem in winter.

LANTANA. Evergreen shrubs with long blooming season. Indoor-outdoor plant. Use outside late spring, summer, fall. Bring inside for frost protection. Good in hanging baskets. Flowers in yellow, lavender, orange, red. Likes sun, standard potting mix, regular watering. Feed occasionally. Too much water, fertilizer cuts down on bloom. Prune frequently to keep compact.

LEMON BALL. See Notocactus mammulosus.

LIGUSTRUM japonicum 'Texanum'. Japanese privet, Waxleaf privet. Evergreen shrub with dense foliage. Dark to medium green, roundish oval, glossy leaves. Use young plants in dish gardens, singly in containers. Prune to keep compact and for shaping. Likes standard potting mix, at least 4 hours of sun, cool temperatures, lots of water.

LILY-OF-THE-NILE. See Agapanthus.

LILY-OF-THE-VALLEY ORCHID. See Odontoglossum pulchellum.

LINDEN, AFRICAN. See Sparmannia.

LIPSTICK PLANT. See Aeschynanthus lobbianus.

LITHOPS. Stoneface. Large succulent family native to South Africa. Shaped like an inverted cone; top resembles a stone with a fissure across the middle. From this fissure emerge a large flower (looks like an ice plant flower) and new leaves. Likes sun, warm temperatures. Plant in equal parts standard potting mix and sharp sand. Water when potting mix is dry to touch in summer; needs no water during winter. (See photo at right.)

LIVISTONA chinensis. Chinese fountain palm. Palm native from China to Australia. Slow growing. Best in large areas. Roundish, bright green, shiny leaves droop at outer edge. Leaf-scarred trunk; old leaves self prune. Likes bright light, average temperatures, standard potting mix, ample water. Fertilize during growing season.

LOBIVIA. Small globular or cylindrical-shaped cactus. Large showy flowers in red, yellow, pink, orange, purplish lilac. Many available species. Likes sun, warm temperatures. Plant in equal parts standard potting mix and sharp sand. Water when potting mix almost dry to touch during growing season, less in winter. Fertilize only during growing season.

LYCASTE. Epiphytic and terrestrial orchids native to Central America. Large pseudobulbs bear 1-3 plaited leaves. Long-lasting, predominantly green flowers; some in pink, white, yellow, brown. Likes cool temperatures (50°-65°), bright light (no direct sun), high humidity. Plant in fibrous loam with

Laelia

Lithops

Lysimachia nummularia

Maranta leuconeura 'Erythroneura'

Maranta leuconeura

enough sphagnum moss and leaf mold to be well drained. Keep potting mix moist except for the period after flowering when watering should be minimal until new growth appears.

L. aromatica. To 16 inches. Bright yellow, fragrant flowers in winter.

L. deppei. To 28 inches. Greenish white flowers dotted brown. Blooms at various times during year.

L. skinneri. To 30 inches. White or pink flowers spotted rose to red in winter.

LYSIMACHIA nummularia. Moneywort, Creeping Jennie. Evergreen creeping plant with long runners. Can be summered outdoors on shaded patio. Good in hanging baskets. Light green, roundish leaves. Yellow flowers form singly at leaf joints in summer. Needs bright light (no direct sun), standard potting mix, average temperatures, some humidity, ample water. Keep compact. (See photo at left.)

MAIDENHAIR FERN. See Adiantum.

MALPIGHIA coccigera. Miniature holly. Evergreen shrub native to tropical America. Small, shiny, dark green leaves with spiny margins, resembles Christmas holly. Pink flowers followed by reddish fruit. Likes filtered light, some humidity, temperatures from 55°-70° (prefers cool nights), standard potting mix. Let soil dry between heavy waterings. Requires occasional pruning.

MAMMILLARIA. Small, cylindrical or globe-shaped cactus either single-stemmed or clustered. Small flowers in red, pink, yellow, white. Likes sun, warm temperatures. Plant in equal parts standard potting mix and sharp sand. Give ample water in summer, less during winter months. Many species available.

M. bocasana. Powder puff cactus. Clustered. Globe-shaped with white hairs. Yellow flowers.

M. hahniana. Old lady cactus. Globular, spiny with long white hairs. Pink to red flowers.

MANDEVILLA 'Alice du Pont' (*Dipladenia*). Evergreen vine needs support to climb or can be trained as a hanger. Dark green, glossy, oval leaves; pink flowers from April through November. Likes bright light (can take some sun), high humidity, regular fertilizing during growing season, standard potting mix, ample water. Pinch young plants for bushy growth. Prune to keep compact.

MAPLE, FLOWERING. See Abutilon.

MARANTA leuconeura. Prayer plant, Rabbit tracks. Foliage plant native to tropical America. Low, bushy growth. Large green leaves with paired brown spots along midrib; spots turn dark green with age. At night, leaves fold together, resembling praying hands (actually the leaves are conserving moisture). Likes filtered light (leaves folding at night and opening again during the day indicate that light is sufficient), high humidity, standard potting mix, regular fertilizing, warm temperatures (above 65°), lots of water. Prune out old or straggly leaves regularly. (See photos, page 70, and at right.)

M. l. 'Erythroneura'. Red-veined prayer plant. Olive green leaves with jagged silver center and red veins.

M. l. 'Kerchoveana'. Undersurface of leaves gray spotted with red.

M. l. 'Massangeana'. Large leaves with prominent veins and pink spots, purple underneath.

MARTHA WASHINGTON GERANIUM. See Pelargonium domesticum.

MATERNITY PLANT. See Kalanchoe daigremoniana.

MEXICAN SNOWBALL. See Echeveria elegans.

MILTONIA. Pansy orchid. Epiphytic orchid native to tropical, subtropical Americas. Long, graceful, light green, bladelike leaves produce a clump of foliage, 10-12 inches tall and wide, above short pseudobulbs. Flowers, single or in clusters, are flat, velvety, resemble pansies; whites, yellows, reds, or blends of these colors are sometimes spotted or patterned. Likes filtered light (no direct sun; can tolerate low light, but dark green foliage indicates too little light), average house temperatures (70°-80°), humidity. Plant in osmunda fiber or ground fir bark. Keep potting mix constantly moist when flower spikes form; water less frequently in winter. Feed weekly with half-strength fertilizer. (See photos at right.)

MIMOSA pudica. Sensitive plant. Tender perennial native to Guatemala. Feathery, grass green leaves fold temporarily when touched, quickly recover. Likes bright light (some sun), warm house temperatures, high humidity, standard potting mix kept moist (avoid overwatering). Good for demonstrating plant movement; children find them fascinating.

MING ARALIA. See Polyscias fruticosa 'Elegans'.

MING FERN. See Asparagus retrofractus.

MISTLETOE FIG. See Ficus diversifolia.

MONEYWORT. See Lysimachia nummularia.

MONSTERA deliciosa (*Philodendron pertusum*). Split-leaf philodendron. Large vining plant native to tropical America. Requires good support to climb. Leathery, dark green leaves, deeply cut and perforated with holes. Long, cordlike roots hanging from stems will root if pushed into the soil; may be removed if preferred. Callalike flowers may form on mature plant. If heat, light, and humidity are high, the flower spike may ripen into edible fruit. Likes bright light (can tolerate from part-time sun to sunless light), standard potting mix, warm temperatures, high humidity, ample water. Feed occasionally. Wipe or wash leaves frequently to clean. Smaller

Maranta leuconeura

Miltonia

Miltonia hybrid

Monstera deliciosa

Neoregelia carolinae 'Tricolor'

leaves or leaves that fail to split indicate poor light, low humidity. (See photo at left.)

MOSAIC PLANT. See Fittonia verschaffeltii.

MOSES-IN-THE-CRADLE, MOSES-IN-THE-BOAT. See Rhoeo spathacea.

MOSS FERN. See Selaginella.

MOTH ORCHID. See Phalaenopsis.

MOTHER FERN. See Asplenium bulbiferum.

MOTHER-IN-LAW PLANT. See Dieffenbachia.

MOTHER-IN-LAW'S TONGUE. See Sansevieria.

MUSA. Banana. Tender perennial tree may form clumps. Dwarf forms (2-5 feet tall) best indoors. May be summered outdoors; protect from wind. Large, broad, shiny green leaves. May develop edible fruit. Good large accent plant. Likes sun, regular fertilizing, warm temperatures, high humidity. Plant in equal parts standard potting mix and peat moss. Give plenty of water.

M. cavendishii (M. nana). To 5-6 feet tall. Leaves 2-3 feet long, bluish green blotched red while young. Edible yellow fruit to 5 inches long.

M. coccinea. To 4 feet tall. Bright green leaves to 3 feet long. Bloom has scarlet bracts, yellow tips.

M. mannii. To 2 feet tall. Stem tinged black. Erect bloom stalk has red bracts, yellow flowers.

M. velutina. To 4 feet tall. Leaves to 3 feet long. Inedible fruit. M. 'Velutina Hybrid' has red markings on leaf edges. Flower stalks with red bracts, yellow flowers.

NATAL PLUM. See Carissa grandiflora.

NEANTHE BELLA. See Chamaedorea elegans.

NEOMARICA northiana. Walking iris, Apostle plant. Rhizomatous perennial native to Brazil. Sword-shaped leaves to 18 inches tall; usually 12 leaves, giving it the nickname "Apostle plant." White, fragrant, irislike flowers marked with violet. Likes bright light, average indoor temperatures and humidity, regular fertilizing, standard potting mix, lots of water.

NEOREGELIA. Epiphytic bromeliads native to tropical America. Many varieties, different in size and color. Rosette growth. Center of plant ("vase") turns crimson at bloom time. Insignificant flowers. Likes bright light, warm temperatures. Plant in osmunda fiber or fir bark. Keep potting mix moist; have "vase" filled with water. (See photo at left.)

N. carolinae 'Tricolor'. Green and white striped leaves. Blue flowers.

N. spectabilis. Fingernail plant. Pale green leaves with red tips. Blue flowers in summer.

NEPHROLEPIS. Sword fern. Easily grown ferns. Sword-shaped fronds with closely-spaced leaflets. Likes bright light (no direct sun), average house temperatures, some humidity, regular fertilizing, good drainage. Plant in equal parts standard potting mix and peat moss. Keep potting mix moist (should be checked daily in warm weather), never let the roots dry out completely. (See photos at right, and on page 74.)

N. cordifolia *(N. exaltata)*. Southern sword fern. Bright green, narrow, upright fronds in tufts to 2-3 feet tall. Leaflets closely spaced, finely toothed.

N. exaltata 'Bostoniense'. Boston fern. Graceful, drooping fronds. A hybrid discovered in Cambridge, Massachusetts in the 1890s. Long-time favorite.

N. e. 'Compacta'. Leaflets toothed. Not readily available.

N. e. 'Fluffy Ruffles'. Upright growing, dark green, very lacy fronds.

N. e. 'Rooseveltii'. Leaflet margins wavy. Tips have deep lobes.

N. e. 'Smithii'. More pyramid-shaped, very lacy (almost feathery) fronds.

N. e. 'Verona'. Very fancy. Each leaflet divided and subdivided.

N. e. 'Whitmanii'. Each leaflet divided with wavy edges.

NEPHTHYTIS. See Syngonium podophyllum.

NERTERA granadensis *(N. depressa)*. Bead plant. Tiny, smooth, rounded leaves form a dense green mat 1-1½ inches high. Small green flowers; bright orange, beadlike fruit. Good in dish gardens, terrariums. Likes filtered light or shade (no direct sun), high humidity, average house temperatures, constant moisture. Plant in light, sandy potting mix.

NERVE PLANT. See Fittonia verschaffeltii.

NICODEMIA diversifolia. Indoor oak. Small branching shrub native to Malagasy. Iridescent, oak-leaf-shaped foliage. Pinch new growth frequently to force branching. Likes bright light, warm temperatures, standard potting mix, ample water. Fertilize during growing season. Prune to keep small.

NIDULARIUM innocentii. Bromeliad native to tropical America. Straplike, olive green leaves with spiny margins; rosette growth. Brilliant red, bractlike leaves form a smaller, nestlike rosette in center. Appropriately, the name *Nidularium* means "bird's nest." White flowers rise out of center in a dense bunch. Likes filtered light, high humidity, average house temperatures. Plant in osmunda fiber or fir bark kept moist.

NORFOLK ISLAND PINE. See Araucaria heterophylla.

NOTOCACTUS. Globe-shaped cactus native to South America. All varieties covered with spines. Flowers in many colors. Likes sun; warm temperatures in summer, cooler (65° or less) during winter. Plant in equal parts standard potting mix and sharp

Nephrolepis exaltata 'Bostoniense'

Nephrolepis exaltata 'Fluffy Ruffles'

Nephrolepis exaltata 'Rooseveltii'

Nephrolepis exaltata 'Smithii'

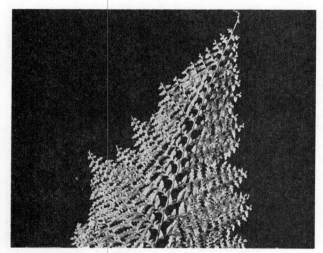
Nephrolepis exaltata 'Verona'

Nephrolepis exaltata 'Whitmanii'

sand. Water when potting mix is dry to touch; give only enough to keep cactus from shrinking in winter.

N. haselbergii. Scarlet ball. Covered with soft, white spines. Red flowers in early spring.

N. mammulosus. Lemon ball. Gray to brown, short-spined, globular, ribbed cactus. Yellow flowers.

N. ottonis. Indian head. Bristly, red-brown spines, glossy green globe. Yellow flowers.

N. scopa. Silver ball. Globular, ribbed, covered with soft, white spines. Yellow flowers.

OAK, INDOOR. See Nicodemia diversifolia.

OCTOPUS TREE. See Brassaia actinophylla.

ODONTOGLOSSUM. Epiphytic orchid native to tropical America. Flat, oval pseudobulbs sheathed by small, leathery leaves with two more leaves on top. Ruffled flowers generally in white, yellow, brown, pink. Likes cool temperatures (45°-65° in winter, as low as possible in summer), bright light (no direct sun), high humidity, good ventilation, regular fertilizing. Plant in osmunda fiber or ground fir bark, let potting mix dry out slightly between waterings. Plants thrive under crowded conditions; keep pot small in relation to plant size.

O. crispum. To 20 inches tall. Flowers white with fringed edges; may be flushed pink, dotted red or brown. Usually blooms in spring, summer.

O. grande. Tiger orchid. To 24 inches. Six-inch yellow flowers with brown strips during fall.

O. harryanum. To 20 inches. Three-inch, wavy, brown flowers marked with yellow, white, purple in summer, early fall.

O. pulchellum. Lily-of-the-Valley orchid. To 10 inches. Waxy, white flowers bloom in spring, have lily-of-the-valley fragrance.

O. uro-skinneri. To 30 inches. One-inch green and brown flowers with lavender edges in early spring.

OLD LADY CACTUS. See Mammillaria hahniana.

OLD MAN CACTUS. See Cephalocereus senilis.

OLIVE, SWEET. See Osmanthus fragrans.

ONCIDIUM. Epiphytic orchids from tropical America. Plant form varies; usually pseudobulbs with leathery leaves (some have pencillike foliage). Flowers either small and numerous or large and solitary. Likes average to cool temperatures, high humidity, good air circulation, at least 4 hours of sun daily (no direct hot sun). Plant in osmunda fiber or ground fir bark; keep potting mix constantly moist except for several weeks following completion of new growth. (See photos at right.)

O. ampliatum. Turtle orchid. To 30 inches. Many red-spotted, yellow flowers in early spring.

O. cheirophorum. To 6 inches. Two narrow leaves from short, rounded pseudobulb. Fragrant, ½-inch, yellow flowers in fall.

O. crispum. To 1-1½-feet tall. Shiny brown, 1½-3-

inch flowers marked with yellow, red; bloom throughout year. Never let potting mix dry out completely.

O. ornithorynchum. To 14 inches. Many tiny lilac flowers in fall or winter.

O. papilio. Butterfly orchid. To 3 feet. Large brown and yellow flowers may bloom all year.

O. sphacelatum. To 3 feet. Many 1-inch, yellow flowers with brown spots in spring, early summer.

O. splendidum. To 3 feet. Three-inch, yellow green and brown flowers in winter.

OPUNTIA. Slow-growing cactus. Many kinds with varied appearance, often bizarre. Most species fall into 1 of 2 rather loose categories: the prickly pears with flat, broad joints and the chollas with cylindrical joints. Rarely blooms indoors. Likes warm temperatures in summer (55°-85°), cool temperatures in winter (around 45°); at least 4 hours of sun daily. Plant in equal parts standard potting mix and sharp sand. Let potting mix dry out completely between waterings; in winter, water only to keep plant from shriveling.

O. basilaris. Beaver tail. Upright, blue-green, compact pads. Pink to carmine flowers.

O. microdasys. Bunny ears. Thin, flat, nearly round pads; velvety, soft green with neatly spaced tufts of short, golden bristles giving a polka dot effect.

O. m. albispina. White bristles. Small new pads atop larger old ones creates plant silhouette of an animal's head. A favorite with children.

ORCHID. Many varieties; most are grown for beautiful flowers. Here are explanations of some growers' terms used in plant descriptions:

Epiphytic. Some orchids are epiphytic, growing high in tree branches in tropical or subtropical jungles, clinging to the bark, but obtaining their nourishment from the air, rain, and whatever decaying vegetable matter they can trap in their root systems.

Flower form. The segments of an orchid flower include 3 sepals and 3 petals. One of the petals, usually the lowest one, is referred to in the descriptions as a lip. This lip is usually larger and more brightly colored than the other segments. Sometimes it is fantastically shaped, with various appendages and markings. It may be folded into a slipperlike "pouch."

Pseudobulb. Epiphytic orchids have thickened stems called pseudobulbs that serve as storage for food and water, making it possible for the plants to survive seasons of drought. These may be short and fat, like bulbs, or erect and slender. They vary from green to brown in color. Leaves may grow along the pseudobulbs or from their tips.

Terrestrial. Terrestrial orchids have their roots growing in a loose, moist soil rich in humus—often in wooded areas but sometimes in open meadows.

Oncidium

Oncidium ampliatum

Ornithogalum caudatum

Osmanthus fragrans

These have no storage organs and require a constant source of moisture and food.

For orchids that will grow indoors, see: *Aerides, Angraecum, Bifrenaria, Brassavola, Brassia maculata, Cattleya, Coelogyne, Cymbidium, Epidendrum, Haemaria discolor, Laelia, Lycaste, Miltonia, Oncidium, Paphiopedilum, Phalaenopsis, Vanda.*

ORCHID CACTUS. See Epiphyllum.

ORNITHOGALUM caudatum. Pregnant onion, False sea onion. Bulb. Strap-shaped, drooping leaves to 2 feet atop a gray-green, smooth-skinned bulb; the greater part of the bulb sits on top of the potting mix. Bulblets form underneath papery outer layer of bulb and swell until they become noticeable bumps, inspiring the nickname "pregnant onion." Eventually the bulblets split the outer layer and fall to the ground, taking root. Tall wands of tiny green and white flowers in April-May. Likes at least 4 hours of sun daily (can tolerate filtered light), standard potting mix, average house temperatures, regular waterings, occasional fertilizing. Failure to water will cause leaf drop; plants recover when watering is resumed. Do not fertilize or water when bulbs go dormant. (See photo at left.)

OSMANTHUS. Evergreen trees or shrubs. Leathery, green foliage. Inconspicuous fragrant flowers. Pinch and prune to keep compact and bushy. Likes at least 4 hours of sun (can tolerate filtered light), standard potting mix, average house temperatures, lots of water. (See photo at left.)

O. fragrans. Sweet olive. Slow-growing. May prune to grow upright. Leaves glossy, medium green, oval; may be toothed or smooth-edged. White flowers with fruity fragrance in spring, early summer. Young plants grow best in filtered light.

O. heterophyllus. False holly. Hollylike foliage. Grows slowly to 3 feet or more. Can tolerate drafts.

OXALIS. Cloverlike leaves. Many species grow from bulbs, tubers. Leaves fold closed at night. Small flowers in pink, white, yellow, rose. Likes a sunny window, standard potting mix, some humidity. Water heavily during growing season.

O. acetosella. Wood sorrel, Shamrock. One of several plants sold as "shamrock."

O. adenophylla. Low, dense growth. Each leaf has 12-22 crinkly, gray-green leaflets. Bell-shaped flowers in lilac pink bloom in late spring.

O. bowiei. Pink or rose flowers in summer. Good in hanging baskets.

O. crassipes. Compact growth. Small, rose pink flowers bloom throughout year.

O. hirta. Upright growth; branching stems gradually fall over under weight of leaves, flowers. Cloverlike leaves on very short stalks. Rose pink flowers in late fall or winter. Plant bulbs in fall. Good in hanging baskets.

O. pes-caprae. Bermuda buttercup. Clusters of bright green, cloverlike leaves (often spotted brown) spring directly from soil in fall. Clusters of bright yellow flowers in winter, spring. Spreads rapidly.

O. purpurea. Large leaves. Rose red, 1-inch flowers in November-March. Spreading habit. Plant bulbs in fall.

OXTONGUE. See Gasteria.

PAINTED LADY. See Echeveria derenbergii.

PAINTED NETTLE. See Coleus blumei.

PALM. A large, widespread, diverse family. Some have single unbranched trunks; others grow in clusters (many stems); a few are dwarf or stemless. Leaves are usually divided into many leaflets, but some have undivided leaves. Most are tropical or subtropical. Indoors, use young plants. Growing plants in pots usually keeps growth slow. Give them potting mix with excellent drainage. Palms usually need little maintenance, making them excellent house plants. For palms to be used indoors, see: *Chamaedorea, Chamaerops humilis, Chrysalidocarpus lutescens, Hedyscepe, Howeia, Livistona chinensis, Phoenix roebelenii, Rhapis.*

PANAMIGA. See Pilea involucrata.

PANDA PLANT. See Kalanchoe tomentosa.

PANDANUS. Screw pine. Native to the South Pacific. Spirally arranged foliage with prickly-edged, spearlike, dark green leaves. Many varieties, some banded with white or silver. Likes standard potting mix, bright light (protect from hot direct sun), warm temperatures, some humidity (likes misting in summer). Water well in summer (drench plant, then let potting mix dry out); rest plant during winter. With age, develops thick, stiltlike, aerial roots around base.

PANSY ORCHID. See Miltonia.

PAPHIOPEDILUM. Lady's slipper. Terrestrial orchid native to tropical regions of Asia. Usually sold as *Cypripedium.* Graceful, arching foliage (no pseudobulbs) either plain green or mottled. Plain-leafed forms usually flower in winter, mottled-leafed forms in summer. Under this name fall the large-flowered hybrids sold commercially for cut flowers. Many flowers shine as if lacquered. Flowers may be white, yellow, green with white stripes, pure green, or a combination of background colors with markings in tan, mahogany brown, maroon, green, white. Mottled-leaf forms need 60°-65° nighttime temperatures, 70°-85° during day. Plain-leafed forms require 55°-65° night temperatures, 60°-75° day temperatures. No rest period, so keep plants moist at all times. Plant in equal parts ground bark and sandy loam. Use smallish pots; *Paphiopedilum* thrives when crowded. Repot yearly after bloom. Likes bright light (no direct sun), some humidity, good air circulation. Use fertilizers only in very weak solutions. (See photos at right.)

Paphiopedilum hybrid

Paphiopedilum hybrid

Pedilanthus tithymaloides

Pelargonium

P. insigne. Green and brown, polished, lady slipper-type flowers on stiff, brown, hairy stems in October-March. Hardy variety.

PAPYRUS, DWARF. See Cyperus haspan.

PARADISE PALM. See Howeia forsteriana.

PARLOR PALM. See Chamaedorea elegans.

PARSLEY PANAX. See Polyscias fruticosa 'Elegans'.

PARTRIDGE-BREAST ALOE. See Aloe variegata.

PASSIFLORA. Passion vine. Indoor-outdoor vining plant. Provide support for upright growth. Nickname comes from manner in which flower parts symbolize elements of the passion of the Lord: the lacy crown could be a halo or a crown of thorns; the five stamens, the five wounds; the ten petallike parts, the ten faithful apostles. Needs pruning. Likes standard potting mix; bright light; average temperatures, watering, fertilizing.

P. alato-caerulea. Best known. Leaves 3 inches long, 3-lobed. Fragrant flowers are white shaded pink and lavender; crown blue or purple. Blooms all summer.

P. caerula. Blue crown passion flower. Flowers greenish white; crown white and purple. Small, oval, orange-colored fruits.

P. manicata. Flowers to 4 inches across; scarlet with narrow, blue crown.

P. racemosa (*P. princeps*). Leathery leaves. Showy deep rose maroon to coral flowers with purple and white crown hang in clusters.

PASSION VINE. See Passiflora.

PATIENT LUCY. See Impatiens walleriana.

PEACOCK FERN. See Selaginella uncinata.

PEACOCK PLANT. See Calathea makoyana.

PEANUT CACTUS. See Chamaecereus silvestri.

PEDILANTHUS tithymaloides. Devil's backbone, Redbird cactus. Succulent. Nicknames come from strange, zigzag stems and small, red, birdlike flowers in spring. Lance-shaped leaves are light green with splashes of red, white, and dark green. 'Nanus' a dwarf variety. Likes light from full sun to semishade, average temperatures and humidity, standard potting mix kept evenly moist. (See photo at left.)

PELARGONIUM. Geranium. Many different flower and leaf forms, some with scented leaves. Flowers in wide range of colors. Keep somewhat potbound for best bloom. When repotting, move to next largest pot size. Likes standard potting mix, a sunny window, warm, dry atmosphere. Water when soil almost dry. Fertilize during active growing season. Pinch out growing tips for bushiness. Don't mist. (See photo at left.)

P. crispum. Lemon-scented geranium. Small, crinkly leaves. Lavender flowers. Dry leaves for closets, potpourris. 'Variegated Prince Rupert' has green and white leaves.

P. domesticum. Lady Washington pelargonium, Martha Washington geranium. Leaves heart-shaped to kidney-shaped, dark green with crinkled margins, unequal sharp teeth. Large, showy flower clusters in white, pinks, red, lavender, purple; many with brilliant blotches, markings of darker colors.

P. fragrans. Nutmeg-scented geranium. Small, roundish, gray-green leaves. Flowers white, pink veins.

P. graveolens. Rose geranium. Leaves dark green, slightly hairy, deeply lobed with each lobe divided and toothed. Small flowers are rose-colored or pink veined with purple. Use leaves in potpourris, sachets, jellies. 'Lady Plymouth' has smaller variegated leaves.

P. hortorum. Most widely grown. Shrubby with succulent stems. Leaves round or kidney-shaped, velvety and hairy, soft to the touch; edges lobed or scalloped with zones of color just inside margins. Large flowers, single or double, in white, pink, rose, red orange, violet.

P. nervosum. Lime-scented geranium. Round, somewhat ruffled, green leaves. Lavender flowers.

P. odoratissimum. Apple-scented geranium. Trailing stems; good in hanging baskets. Roundish, ruffled leaves. White flowers in clusters.

P. peltatum. Ivy geranium. Trailing stems; good in hanging baskets. Glossy, bright green, ivylike leaves with pointed lobes. Flowers, single or double, in white, pink, rose, red, lavender; two upper petals blotched or striped.

P. tomentosum. Peppermint-scented geranium. Large, lobed leaves, velvety to touch. Small white flowers in clusters. Good in hanging baskets.

PELLAEA. Cliff brake. Small ferns with detailed foliage. Likes standard potting mix with good drainage, filtered light, some humidity. Give lots of water but don't let pot sit in it. (See photo at right.)

P. rotundifolia. Button fern, Roundleaf fern. Nearly round, dark green leaflets evenly spaced. Good contrast with lacier ferns.

P. viridis. *(P. adiantoides).* Long fronds to 2 feet. Fresh green, oval to lance-shaped leaflets on brownish black stems.

PELLIONIA. Trailing plant native to tropical Asia. Variegated oval foliage. Good for hanging baskets or train on support as a climber. Likes bright light, average house temperatures, high humidity, ample water.

P. daveauana. Brownish leaves with pale green markings in leaf center.

P. pulchra. Oval, gray-green leaves with patterned veins in browns, purples.

PEPEROMIA. Evergreen, often succulent, plants with a variety of interesting foliage. Good companion plant in dish gardens. Likes filtered light or a north (sunless) exposure (protect plant from direct sun), standard potting mix with good drainage, high

Pellaea viridis

Peperomia 'Astrid'

Peperomia caperata 'Emerald Ripple'

Peperomia obtusifolia 'Variegata'

Peperomia polybotrya

humidity, warm temperatures (will tolerate less), not too much water. (See photos, page 79, and at left.)

P. 'Astrid'. Apple green, pointed, succulent leaves; compact growth. Long, white flower spikes.

P. caperata 'Emerald Ripple'. Heart-shaped, deeply veined, rich green leaves; short reddish stalks. 'Little Fantasy' a miniature variety.

P. fosteri. Trailing variety with reddish stems. Succulent, dark green leaves with lighter veins.

P. magnoliaefoliae. Almost round leaves with yellow variegation.

P. metallica. Erect, dark red stems with narrow, waxy leaves of copper with a metallic luster and silver green band down leaf center.

P. obtusifolia. Round, dark green, succulent leaves. 'Minima' is miniature form. 'Variegata' leaves with creamy white margins, light and dark green markings.

P. polybotrya. Shieldlike, dark green, succulent leaves with white flower stalks.

P. rotundifolia. Slender, trailing stems; tiny, green, round leaves. Good as ground cover in dish gardens.

P. sandersii. Watermelon peperomia. Round leaves with gray-silver, curved stripes on long stems.

PEPPER, ORNAMENTAL. See Capsicum annuum.

PHALAENOPSIS. Moth orchid. Epiphytic orchids native to tropical Asia. Thick, broad, leathery leaves; no pseudobulbs. White and pink-flowered species most widely grown; yellow and multicolored varieties also available. Likes shade (no direct sun), average to warm house temperatures (60° is minimum), high humidity (at least 60%). Plant in osmunda fiber or ground fir bark. *Phalaenopsis* should never dry out completely but can't stand overwatering. Repot infrequently. Not for beginners.

PHILODENDRON. Evergreen vines and shrubs. Tough, durable plants grown for their attractive, leathery, usually glossy leaves. Two main classes: arborescent (and relatively hardy) and vining (or self-heading and tender). Arborescent *Philodendrons* become big plants with large leaves and sturdy, self-supporting trunks. Will require more space than most house plants. May be summered outdoors. Vining or self-heading *Philodendrons* are only house plants. Vining types need support. Support can be almost anything, but certain water-absorbent columns (sections of tree fern stems, wire and sphagnum moss "totem poles," slabs of redwood bark) serve well because they can be kept moist. Self-heading types form short, broad plant with sets of leaves radiating out from central point. All *Philodendrons* like standard potting mix with good drainage, average house temperatures, good light but no direct sun, some humidity. All like ample water but will not tolerate soggy soil. Fertilize frequently with light fertilizer mixtures. Aerial roots form on some kinds; push them into the soil or cut them off. Callalike flowers may appear on old plants grown in perfect environment. Flower bracts are usually green, white, or reddish. Most drop lower leaves, exposing stems. Leafy top of plant can be air layered and repotted or plant can be cut back to stub to start over. (See photos at right.)

P. 'Hastatum'. Vining. Fairly fast, open growth. Leaves 1 foot long, arrow-shaped, rich green. Subject to leaf spot if kept too warm, moist.

P. 'Mandaianum'. Vining. Leaves arrow-shaped, 12-15 inches long, dark green above, maroon underneath. Stalks maroon.

P. oxycardium (*P. cordatum*). Vining. Most common. Deep green, heart-shaped leaves usually 5 inches or less in length on young plants. Cut stems will live and grow in water for some time. Plants will climb or trail.

P. panduraeforme. Fiddle-leaf philodendron. Vining. Fairly fast climber with rich green, 10-inch leaves oddly lobed to resemble a violin. Sparse foliage on older plants; best planted in multiples.

P. pertusum. Split-leaf philodendron. (See *Monstera deliciosa, page 71*).

P. radiatum (*P. dubium*). Vining. Slow to climb. Nine-inch, deep green leaves deeply cut into many narrow, spidery segments. More delicate in effect than *Monstera,* much slower growing.

P. selloum. Arborescent. Leaves to 3 feet, deeply cut. Variety 'Lundii' is more compact.

P. sodiroi. Vining or self-heading. Heart-shaped, olive green leaves mottled with silver. Staked plant leaves may become larger than those unsupported.

PHOENIX roebelenii. Pigmy date palm. Palm native to Laos. Fine-leafed, small-scale plant; stem grows slowly to 6 feet. Curved leaves from dense crown. Likes standard potting mix with extra leaf mold or humus, average to warm house temperatures, lots of water. Does best in shade or filtered light but not successful in dark corners.

PHYLLITIS scolopendrium. Hart's tongue fern. Native to Europe, eastern United States. Unusual fern with glossy, undivided, strap-shaped fronds. Some dwarf varieties. Likes moisture, shade, high humidity, cool temperatures.

PHYLLOSTACHYS aurea. Golden bamboo. Indoor-outdoor plant. Dense foliage on stems 6-10 feet tall. Not recommended for year-round indoor culture. Give cool temperatures, bright light. Keep potting mix constantly moist. Fertilize regularly and repot every 2-3 years. When moving indoors or out, avoid sudden changes in light, temperatures.

P. nigra. Black bamboo. Stems vary from pure black to olive-dotted black. Grows to 4-8 feet tall.

P. viridis. Curving tall stems (can reach 20 feet), with ferny growth at base. Good accent for entryways.

PIGGY-BACK PLANT. See Tolmiea menziesii.

PIGMY DATE PALM. See Phoenix roebelenii.

Philodendron 'Mandaianum'

Philodendron selloum

Pilea cadierei

Pilea microphylla

Pilea 'Silver Tree'

PILEA. Juicy-stemmed plants with inconspicuous flowers. Become leggy with too much shade. Likes standard potting mix with good drainage, bright light, average to warm house temperatures, regular fertilizing (once a month) during growing season. Water thoroughly but don't water again until soil surface is dry. (See photos at left.)

P. cadierei. Aluminum plant. Erect growth with showy, silver-flecked leaves. 'Minima' is dwarf variety.

P. depressa. Baby's tears. Bright, apple green, tiny, roundish leaves; creeping growth. Good as ground cover in dish gardens, terrariums.

P. involucrata. Panamiga, Panamigo. Glossy roundish oval, bronze green leaves with purplish undersides, heavily veiled in seersucker effect.

P. 'Moon Valley.' Erect-growing hybrid. Almost quilted texture. Greenish brown leaves.

P. microphylla. Artillery plant. Tiny, thick, bright green leaves in fernlike sprays. Prune to keep compact. Nickname comes from habit of "forcibly discharging pollen" (quote from *The Standard Cyclopedia of Horticulture* by L. H. Bailey).

P. nummulariaefolia. Creeping Charlie. Creeping habit; small, round, slightly hairy leaves.

P. 'Silver Tree'. Dark, olive green leaves with silvery strip down middle.

PINE, FERN. See Podocarpus gracilior.

PINE, YEW. See Podocarpus macrophyllus.

PINEAPPLE. See Ananas.

PINK POLK-A-DOT PLANT. See Hypoestes sanguinolenta.

PISONIA. See Heimerliodendron brunonianum 'Variegatum.'

PITCHER PLANT, CALIFORNIA. See Darlingtonia.

PITTOSPORUM tobira. Thick, shiny, leathery leaves rounded at ends, arranged in whorls. Clusters of creamy white flowers in early spring have fragrance of orange blossoms. Normally an outdoor shrub; use immature form and prune heavily for indoor use. Likes standard potting mix, temperatures below 75°, some humidity, light that may vary from semi-sunny to semi-shady, lots of water.

PLATYCERIUM. Staghorn fern. Odd epiphytic fern from tropical regions. Two kinds of fronds: sterile ones (flat, pale green aging to tan and brown, they support plant and accumulate organic matter to help feed it) and fertile fronds (forked, resembling deer antlers for which they are nicknamed). Can be summered outdoors on shaded patios. In nature it grows on trees; grow it on slabs of bark or tree fern stem; occasionally used in hanging baskets. Likes bright light, high humidity (mist frequently), average to cool temperatures. Grow in organic matter kept moist at all times. Give them lots of space.

P. bifurcatum. Native to Australia, New Guinea. Fertile fronds clustered, gray-green, to 3 feet long.

P. grande. From Australia. Both fertile and sterile fronds forked, the former broad and divided like moose antlers. Do not overwater.

PLECTRANTHUS. Swedish ivy. Trailing perennial from Africa with round, thick, almost succulent leaves. Tiny white flowers on upright spikes. Likes standard potting mix; average temperatures, moisture, and humidity. Tolerates dim light. Fast growing. Good in hanging baskets. (See photo at right.)

P. australis. Shiny, dark green leaves.

P. coleoides 'Marginatus'. Dark green leaves with white, toothed, scalloped edges.

P. oertendahlii. Apple green leaves with silver veins, purple underneath. Pinkish flowers.

PLUME ASPARAGUS. See Asparagus densiflorus 'Myeri'.

PODOCARPUS. Evergreen trees and shrubs; slow growing. Will stay compact if pruned when young. Indoor-outdoor plant. Adaptable to many conditions. Likes filtered light (shaded patio outdoors; will tolerate some sun), standard potting mix, cool temperatures below 75°, some humidity, ample water.

P. gracilior (*P. elongatus*). Fern pine. Upright, willowy, graceful growth. Leaves dense, bluish or grayish green in color.

P. macrophyllus. Yew pine. Bright green leaves. Narrow upright growth. Prune to shape.

P. m. maki. Shrubby yew pine. Smaller, slower growing than *P. macrophyllus*.

P. nagi. Slow-growing. Drooping branches on erect stem. Leaves leathery, smooth, sharp-pointed. More treelike in youth than other *Podocarpus*.

POINSETTIA. See Euphorbia pulcherrima.

POLYPODIUM aureum. Hare's foot fern. Fern native to tropical America. Good in hanging baskets. Leathery fronds with toothed leaves. Heavy, brown, hairy, creeping rhizomes that resemble animals' feet, giving them their nickname. Likes filtered light, potting mix high in organic matter, average temperatures, humidity (mist often—prefers to be kept moist).

POLYSCIAS. Plants related to the *Aralia* family but native to tropical Asia and Polynesia (true *Aralias* are native to China). Touchy, slow-growing, sensitive to cold. Needs bright light, regular fertilizing, standard potting mix, high humidity (likes misting). Put in warmest spot in house; keep free of drafts. Water well about once a week when soil is dry to touch. (See photo at right.)

P. balfouriana. Round, slightly scalloped, solid green leaves.

P. b. 'Marginata'. Round scalloped leaves with white margin. Tolerates either sun or shade.

Plectranthus australis

Polyscias fruticosa 'Elegans'

Pteris ensiformis 'Victoriae'

Pteris quadriaurita 'Argyraea'

P. b. 'Pennockii'. Same foliage form as *P. balfouriana*; leaf color is white to pale green with irregular green spots.

P. filicifolia. Bright green, fernlike foliage; leaf segments larger than *P. fruticosa* and doubly divided.

P. fruticosa 'Elegans'. Ming aralia, Parsley panax. Parsleylike foliage on woody stem.

P. guilfoylei 'Victoriae'. Thin, leathery, curled leaves with white toothed edges.

P. paniculata 'Variegata'. Roundish, light green leaves with dark green, toothed edges.

POLYSTICHUM. Fern with dark green fronds that form symmetrical plants. Likes standard potting mix with added humus, shade, ample water, average indoor temperatures and humidity.

P. tsus-simense. Dwarf variety to 8 inches with leathery, dark green fronds.

POMEGRANATE, DWARF. See Punica granatum 'Nana'.

POTHOS. See Rhaphidophora aurea.

POWDER PUFF CACTUS. See Mammillaria bocasana.

PREGNANT ONION. See Ornithogalum.

PRAYER PLANT. See Maranta leuconeura.

PROPELLER PLANT. See Crassula cultrata.

PTERIS. Brake, Table fern, Ribbon fern, Victoria fern. Tropical ferns best known for forked and crested, green or variegated fronds. Many varieties. Likes filtered light (can tolerate shade), cool temperatures, humidity, ample water. (See photos at left.)

P. cretica. To 1½ feet. A few large, narrow leaflets. Many forms, some variegated, some with forked or crested fronds.

P. ensiformis 'Victoriae'. Silvery white fronds edged in dark green.

P. quadriaurita 'Argyraea'. Silver fern. Native to India. Tall fronds rather coarsely divided, heavily marked with white.

PUNICA granatum 'Nana'. Dwarf Pomegranate. Dense shrub to 3 feet high. Glossy, bright green leaves, almost evergreen. Orange red single flowers followed by small, dry, red fruit. Likes sun, warm temperatures, standard potting mix with good drainage, average amounts of water.

PURPLE HEART. See Setcreasea purpurea.

QUEEN'S TEARS. See Billbergia nutans.

RABBIT TRACKS. See Maranta leuconeura.

RABBIT'S FOOT FERN. See Davallia fejeensis.

RAINBOW CACTUS. See Echinocereus dasyacanthus.

RATTAN PALM. See Rhapis humilis.

RATTLESNAKE PLANT. See Calathea insignis.

REBUTIA. Cactus native to tropical America. Small barrel shape. Flowers in spring. Likes sun, average house temperatures, more water than most cactus except during winter rest, when it needs cool temperatures (55°) and somewhat dry conditions.

R. kupperiana. Small gray globe; red flowers.

R. miniscula. Bright green globe; large red flowers.

R. senilis. Fire crown. Dark green plant covered with mass of snow white spines; abundant red flowers.

RECHSTEINERIA. Tuberous plants related to African violets. Compact, broad-leafed growth. Narrow, tubular, mostly red flowers. Likes warm temperatures (65° at night, 70° during the day), high humidity, bright light (no direct hot summer sun), regular fertilizing during growing season. Plant in packaged African violet potting mix. Generously water when soil surface dries out; never let roots dry out. During winter rest period, gradually withhold water until leaves turn yellow; then stop watering until they dry out. Water only enough to keep tubers plump. When new growth starts (or after 3 months dormancy), resume watering and fertilizing.

R. cardinalis. Most common. Broad, heart-shaped, fuzzy leaves grow compactly in opposite pairs. Red flowers in summer. Can have flowers at Christmas if tubers are started in fall.

R. leucotricha. Brazilian edelweiss. Silvery leaves covered with white hairs. Salmon-red flowers.

R. verticillata. Whorls of leaves encircle stems with an umbrella effect. Purple-spotted, pink flowers in clusters.

REDBIRD CACTUS. See Pedilanthus.

RED-HOT CATTAIL. See Acalypha hispida.

REX BEGONIA. See Begonia rex-cultorum.

RHAPHIDOPHORA aurea (*Scindapsus aureus, Pothos aureus*). Devil's ivy, Silver pothos. Evergreen, perennial climbers related to *Philodendron*, similar in appearance. Oval, leathery leaves with pale white or yellow splotches. Train to climb or trail. Good in hanging baskets. Likes standard potting mix, good light, regular watering, fertilizer; will tolerate adverse conditions. (See photo at right.)

RHAPIS. Lady Palm. Fan palm that forms bamboo-like clumps with deep green foliage. Trunks covered with a net of dark, fibrous leaf sheaths. Slow growing; excellent container palm. Likes semi-shade (can tolerate some sun or poor light), average house temperatures and humidity, regular fertilizing (weak feedings monthly), standard potting mix. Water frequently. (See photos at right.)

R. excelsa. Slow grower to about 12 feet. Resists poor light, dust, drought.

R. humilis. Rattan palm, Slender lady palm. Tall to about 18 feet. Gives graceful tropical air. Larger, longer leaves than *R. excelsa,* less tolerant of sun.

Rhaphidophora aurea

Rhapis excelsa

Rhapis humilis

Rhoeo spathacea

Saintpaulia ionantha

RHIPSALIDOPSIS gaertneri (*Schlumbergera gaertneri*). Easter cactus. Epiphytic cactus with drooping branches native to the tropics. Flowers to 3 inches long, bright red, upright or horizontal rather than drooping. Blooms April, May, often repeats in September. Other varieties in pinks, reds. Plant in rich, porous soil with leaf mold and sand. Likes frequent watering, fertilizing as often as every 7-10 days, filtered light, some humidity.

RHIPSALIS paradoxa. Rice cactus. Epiphytic cactus with hanging branches, no spines. Flat, green leaves with sawtooth edges. Tiny white flowers in winter, followed by red berries. Good in hanging baskets. Likes shade or filtered light (not a sun lover), high humidity, rich, porous potting mix. Stop watering in early winter before flowering begins.

RHOEO spathacea (*R. discolor*). Moses-in-the-cradle, Moses-in-the-boat. Perennial. Sword-shaped, rather erect leaves are dark green with deep purple underneath. Interesting flowers; small, white, 3-petaled, they are crowded into boat-shaped bracts down among the leaves, giving plant its nickname. Tolerant plant adapts well to adverse conditions. Likes standard potting mix, average house temperatures and humidity, light from high to low ranges, regular to casual watering. 'Vittata' leaves striped red and yellowish green. (See photo at left.)

RHOICISSUS capensis (*Cissus capensis*). Evergreen grape. Leaves roundish to kidney-shaped, scallop-toothed, deeply lobed. New growth, both stem and leaves, rusty with red hairs. Mature leaves are light green tinged coppery, with rusty hairs beneath. Likes standard potting mix, regular watering, average house conditions; tolerant of most indoor light.

RIBBON FERN. See Pteris.

RIBBON PLANT. See Dracaena sanderiana.

RICE CACTUS. See Rhipsalis paradoxa.

ROHDEA japonica. Perennial grown for dense clump of evergreen foliage. Leaves broadly strap-shaped, usually arched and recurving, dark green to 2 feet long, 3 inches wide. Cream-colored flowers on short spike, followed by red berries. Rhizomatous. Old plants have many foliage clumps. Tough indoor plant. Likes filtered light, standard potting mix, occasional watering, average house conditions.

ROSA chinensis 'Minima'. Miniature rose. Tiny roses grow to 6 inches; they are not dwarf forms of larger roses but a separate strain. Many varieties available in wide range of colors. Grow in any light conditions; can tolerate some sun. Likes standard potting mix with good drainage, lots of water (best to water in morning to avoid mildew), regular fertilizing, high humidity. Aphids, red spider, mildew common problems. Needs constant maintenance when blooming; prune, remove spent blooms.

ROSARY VINE. See Ceropegia woodii.

ROSE, MINIATURE. See Rosa.

RUBBER PLANT. See Ficus elastica.

RUELLIA makoyana. Trailing velvet plant. Native to Brazil. Low, spreading plant with small, velvety, olive green leaves with purple shadings, silvery veins. Likes high humidity, constant moisture, filtered light, daytime temperatures above 65°, standard potting mix with extra humus. Good in terrariums.

SAGO PALM. See Cycas revoluta.

SAINTPAULIA ionantha. African violet. Evergreen perennial native to Africa. Probably the most popular house plant in the United States. Fuzzy, heart-shaped, dark green leaves with smooth edges grow in rosettes. Pale lavender flowers in clusters of 3 or more. Hybrids and named varieties have leaves that are plain or scalloped, green or variegated; flowers are purple, violet, pink, white, cerise, or variegated. Likes very bright light (can take some sun during fall, winter, spring; will grow under artificial light), high humidity, average house temperatures (never below 60°), good air circulation. Plant in packaged African violet potting mix. Water thoroughly from top or bottom with room temperature water; let soil surface become dry between waterings. Don't let water sit in saucer for more than 2 hours. Use smallish pots; African violets bloom best with crowded roots. Feed regularly once every 2-4 weeks (there are commercial fertilizers formulated especially for African violets: follow label directions carefully); be sure soil is moist before feeding. For more information, see the *Sunset* book *How to Grow African Violets*. (See photo, page 86.)

SANSEVIERIA. Bowstring hemp, Snake plant, Mother-in-law's tongue. Evergreen perennial succulent native to Africa, India. Thick, patterned leaves grow in clusters and radiate up and out from base, range in shape from short, blunt triangles to long swords. First nickname comes from use of tough fibers in leaves as bowstrings; second comes from banding or mottling on leaves that causes them to resemble snakeskin; third probably comes from toughness of leaves and plants' persistence under neglect. Clusters of greenish white flowers seldom appear. Likes standard potting mix, average house conditions. Light may vary from bright to low. Water thoroughly but infrequently. Tolerates dry air, uneven temperatures, capricious watering. (See photos at right.)

S. 'Hahnii'. Broad, fleshy, 6-inch, dark green leaves cross-banded with irregular silvery markings. Good in small pots, dish gardens.

S. trifasciata. *(S. zeylanica).* Leaves 1-4 feet long, 2 inches or more wide; fleshy, dark green, banded with silvery gray. Variety 'Laurentii' is best known.

Sansevieria 'Hahnii'

Sansevieria trifasciata 'Laurentii'

Saxifraga stolonifera 'Tricolor'

SASA palmata. Palmate bamboo. Indoor-outdoor plant. Handsome, unbamboolike, broad leaves spread like fingers from stems. Grows 4-5 feet tall. Not recommended for year-round indoor culture but can spend extended periods indoors in containers. Give cool temperatures, bright light. Keep potting mix on the dry side to restrain growth. Fertilize regularly and repot every 2-3 years. Avoid sudden changes in light, temperatures.

SAXIFRAGA stolonifera *(S. sarmentosa).* Strawberry geranium, Strawberry begonia. Creeping perennial native to China, Japan. Forms runners like those of strawberry plants, producing new plantlets at stem ends. Nearly round, fuzzy, white-veined, green leaves with pink underneath. White flowers in clusters on tall stems. Good in hanging baskets. Likes filtered light, standard potting mix, cool temperatures, some humidity, considerable moisture. (See photos at left and on page 89.)

S. s. 'Tricolor'. Green leaves liberally edged in white with pink underneath.

SCHEFFLERA. See Brassaia actinophylla.

SCHLUMBERGERA. Epiphytic cactus (cactus that lives in trees like certain orchids) native to tropics. Plants often confused in nursery trade; many hybrids, selections differ in color. Plant in rich, porous soil with plenty of leaf mold, sand. Likes bright light, humidity, average house temperatures, frequent watering and fertilizing (feed as often as every 7-10 days). To ensure bloom, give plants a rest in fall; keep cool, dry, and give 12 hours of constant darkness. (See photo, back cover.)

S. bridgesii *(Zygocactus truncatus).* Christmas cactus. Nature plant may be 3 feet across, with arching drooping branches made up of flattened, scalloped, smooth, bright green, spineless joints. Many-petaled, tubular, rosy purplish red flowers around Christmas.

S. gaertneri. See *Rhipsalidopsis gaertneri.*

S. truncata *(Zygocactus truncatus).* Crab cactus. Joints 1-2 inches long, sharply toothed, with 2 large teeth at end of last joint. Short-tubed flowers with spreading, pointed, scarlet petals. Blooms Nov.-Mar. Many varieties in white, pink, salmon, orange.

SCINDAPSUS. See Rhaphidophora aurea.

SCREW PINE. See Pandanus.

SEA URCHIN CACTUS. See Echinopsis.

SEDUM. Stonecrop. Succulents that come from many parts of the world and vary in hardiness and growing needs. Some tiny and trailing, others upright. Fleshy leaves highly variable in size, shape, color; evergreen varieties best indoors. Plant in equal parts standard potting mix and sharp sand. Likes bright light. (See photo page 89.)

S. adolphii. Short, fleshy, yellow-green leaves tinged red.

S. brevifolium. Native to Europe, North Africa. Tiny, slow growing, tightly packed, fleshy leaves, gray-white flushed red. Flowers pinkish or white. Sunburns in hot dry spots. Needs good drainage.

S. dasyphyllum. Blue-gray leaves; hairy white flowers.

S. morganianum. Donkey tail, Burro tail. Can be summered outdoors. Long trailing stems to 3-4 feet. Thick, fleshy, light gray-green leaves overlapping on stem, giving a braided or ropelike effect. Good in hanging baskets. Likes filtered light. Water freely (needs good drainage); feed 2-3 times during summer.

S. multiceps. Miniature "tree" form with needle-like, dark green leaves; yellow flowers.

S. stahlii. Coral beads. Native to Mexico. Trailing growth. Reddish-brown leaves set closely together on stem. Yellow flowers in summer or fall.

SEERSUCKER PLANT. See Geogenanthus.

SELAGINELLA. Moss fern, Spike moss. Branching, mosslike plant is taller and fluffier than real moss. Creeping growth. Good as ground cover in terrariums, dish gardens. Can trail in hanging baskets. Likes shade, standard potting mix, high humidity, lots of water. (See photo at right.)

S. kraussiana. Dwarf with bright green leaves.

S. k. 'Aurea'. Yellow-green in color.

S. k. brownii. Club moss. Slow spreading. Smallest form about 1 inch. Pale green in color.

S. uncinata. Peacock fern. Leaves of iridescent metallic blue-green.

SEMPERVIVUM. Houseleek. Evergreen perennial succulent with tightly-packed rosettes of leaves. Little offsets cluster around parent rosette. Star-shaped flowers in clusters in white, yellowish, pink, red, greenish; summer blooming. Blooming rosettes die after setting seed, but offsets continue. Plant in equal parts standard potting mix and sharp sand. Likes sun, good drainage, lots of water in summer.

S. arachnoideum. Cobweb houseleek. Rosettes of gray-green, hairy leaves laced together with fine hairs, giving a cobweb-covered appearance. Bright red flowers; seldom blooms.

S. montanum. Tightly-packed, tiny leaf rosettes.

S. tectorum. Hen and chickens. Gray-green rosettes that quickly spread. Leaves tipped red-brown, bristle-pointed. Red flowers.

SENECIO. Perennials related to the daisy; some succulent. Mostly hardy, adaptable to house conditions. Likes standard potting mix, sun or bright light; average watering, house temperatures, humidity.

S. mikanioides. German ivy. Vining growth; good in hanging baskets. Should be evergreen indoors (can be deciduous in all but mildest climates). Roundish, ivylike leaves with 5-7 sharply-pointed lobes. Small yellow flowers in winter. Prune to control size.

Saxifraga stolonifera

Sedum brevifolium

Selaginella kraussiana

Sinningia speciosa

Smithiantha cinnabarina

S. rowleyanus. String of beads. Succulent. Trailing or hanging stems set with ½-inch, spherical, green leaves that resemble beads. Good in hanging baskets. Small, white, carnation-scented flowers.

SENSITIVE PLANT. See Mimosa pudica.

SENTRY PALM. See Howeia belmoreana.

SETCREASEA purpurea. Purple heart. Perennial to 1 foot or more. May lean or droop. Leaves narrowly oval to pointed, strongly shaded purple — particularly underneath. Pale to deep purple flowers unimportant. Provide bright light (some sun) for good leaf color, standard potting mix, normal house plant care.

SHAMROCK. See Oxalis acetosella.

SHRIMP PLANT. See Beloperone guttata.

SICKLE-THORN ASPARAGUS. See Asparagus falcatus.

SIDERASIS fuscata. Rosette of oval green leaves with velvety red hairs and a white midrib; purple underneath. Likes standard potting mix with extra humus added, cool to average temperatures (60°-70°), bright light. Water when soil surface dries out.

SILK OAK. See Grevillea robusta.

SILVER DOLLAR. See Crassula arborescens.

SILVER FERN. See Pteris quadriaurita 'Argyraea'.

SINNINGIA speciosa (*Gloxinia speciosa*). Gloxinia. Tuberous plant native to South American tropics. Related to African violets. Tubers usually available December-March. Large, oblong, dark green, toothed, fuzzy leaves to 6 inches or more. Large flowers, velvety, bell-shaped, ruffled on edges, in purple, blue, violet, pink, red, white. Some flowers have dark spots or blotches. Plant tubers in packaged African violet potting mix with sand added; 3 parts mix to 1 part sand. Tuberous plants normally go dormant; when plant stops growing (no new leaves or flowers), withhold water until leaves turn yellow; then stop watering so they will dry out. Dormancy lasts for 1½-3 months; give only enough water to prevent tuber from shriveling and soil from completely drying out. Store at about 60°. When new growth begins, repot or plant tuber 1 inch below soil surface (be sure indented top side faces up). Water moderately until roots are established; then water generously. Allow soil surface to dry out between waterings. Likes high humidity, temperatures from 65°-75°, bright light, regular fertilizing every 2-4 weeks during growing season. (See photo at left.)

SMITHIANTHA (*Naegelia*). Temple bells. Native to mountain regions in Mexico, Guatemala. Grows from rhizomes. Heart-shaped leaves with densely hairy, velvety leaves. Bell-shaped flowers that hang down like bells in wide range of colors and color combinations. Likes coolish temperatures (60°-70°), filtered light, high humidity, lots of water (never let soil dry out completely). When plants go dormant (usually in fall), withhold water and let rhizomes dry out; store in cool place for about 3 months. When new growth starts, repot and return to bright light, regular watering. Plant in packaged African violet potting mix. (See photo, page 90.)

S. cinnabarina. Green leaves with velvety red hairs; leaves appear red. Brick red flowers.

S. multiflora. Velvety green leaves, lighter green underneath. Cream or white-colored flowers.

S. zebrina. Leaves with veins marked brown or purple. Red flowers with red-spotted, yellow throats.

SNAKE PLANT. See Sansevieria.

SNOWFLAKE TREE. See Trevesia.

SOLANUM pseudo-capsicum. Jerusalem cherry. Evergreen shrub native to tropics. Deep green, smooth, shiny leaves to 4 inches. White flowers followed by red fruit (rarely yellow) like miniature tomatoes, October-December. Colorful at Christmas time. Fruits may be poisonous. Usually grown as an annual. Pinch and prune frequently to control growth. Many dwarf varieties. Likes bright light (some sun), average temperatures, standard potting mix, regular watering and fertilizing.

SOLEIROLIA soleirolii (*Helxine soleirolii*). Baby's tears, Angel's tears. Native to Corsica, Sardinia. Creeping, mosslike plants with tiny, round, medium green leaves that form a thick mat. Inconspicuous flowers. Fast growing; pruning encourages more growth. Likes shade or filtered light, standard potting mix, cool temperatures, high humidity, ample water (won't tolerate standing in water). Use in small containers or as ground cover in terrariums, dish gardens.

SPARMANNIA africana. African linden. Evergreen shrub, tree, native to South Africa. Forms into many trunks from base. Leaves to 9 inches, light green, heavily veined, broad, angled, velvety with coarse hairs. Clusters of white flowers in midwinter. Likes standard potting mix, either sun or shade, average house temperatures, some humidity, ample water and fertilizing. Prune to control size and prevent legginess. Susceptible to spider mite.

SPATHIPHYLLUM. White flag. Evergreen perennial. Leaf stalks rise directly from soil. Dark green, large, oval leaves narrow to a point. White flowers resemble calla lilies. Blooms readily indoors. Likes bright light (no direct hot sun), high humidity, frequent watering, regular fertilizing, loose, fibrous potting mix. Commonly available: *S. wallisii, S.* 'Mauna Loa', *S.* 'Clevelandii'; all similar in appearance. (See photo at right.)

Spathiphyllum 'Clevelandii'

Strelitzia reginae

Streptocarpus

SPIDER ORCHID. See Brassia maculata.

SPIDER PLANT. See Chlorophytum comosum.

SPIKE MOSS. See Selaginella.

SPLIT-LEAF PHILODENDRON. See Monstera.

SQUIRREL'S FOOT FERN. See Davallia trichomanoides.

STAGHORN FERN. See Platycerium.

STAPELIA. Starfish flower, Carrion flower. Succulent resembling cactus with clumps of 4-sided, spineless stems. Can be summered outdoors. Flowers in summer are large, fleshy, star-shaped with 5 points; usually have an elaborate circular disk in center. Most flowers smell like carrion; not too offensive outdoors. Needs a cool, dry rest period in winter. Likes filtered light, standard potting mix, average house conditions. Moderate watering during growing season.

    S. gigantia. Novelty with 9-inch stems. Flowers 10-16 inches across, brown-purple marked yellow with fringed edges.

    S. variegata. Most common. Stems to 6 inches. Flowers 3 inches across, yellow heavily spotted and barred with dark purple-brown. Many hybrids and color variants. Unscented flowers.

STAR OF BETHLEHEM. See Campanula.

STEPHANOTIS floribunda. Madagascar jasmine. Evergreen vine native to Malagasy. Can be summered outdoors. Leaves glossy, dark green, waxy, to 4 inches. Funnel-shaped flowers white, waxy, very fragrant, in open clusters. Outdoors, blooms June through summer; grown indoors and given proper rest by some drying out, will bloom 6 weeks after resuming growth. Outdoors, keep roots in shade, tops in filtered sun. Indoors, likes bright light (no direct sun), some support (frame or trellis), liberal water and fertilizer. If summered outdoors, let dry out somewhat before bringing indoors. Scale, mealybug common pests.

STONECROP. See Sedum.

STONEFACE. See Lithops.

STRAWBERRY BEGONIA. See Saxifraga.

STRELITZIA reginae. Bird of paradise. Can be summered outdoors. Tropical evergreen perennial. Leathery, long-stalked, blue-green leaves to 1½ feet in clumps. Large, crowded clumps bloom best. Orange, blue, and white flowers on long, stiff stems bloom intermittently throughout the year; resemblance to tropical birds gives nickname. Likes sun (light shade in hot areas), average to warm temperatures, frequent heavy fertilizing, regular waterings. (See photo at left.)

STREPTOCARPUS. Cape primrose. Evergreen perennials native to South Africa. Related to African violets. Many species that vary in size, shapes of leaves, flowers. Leaves large, fleshy, sometimes velvety. Flowers trumpet-shaped with long tube and spreading mouth, fall-winter bloom. Buy plants or grow from seed. Likes cool temperatures (55°-60°), bright light (no direct sun), packaged African violet potting mix. Keep moist. Hybrids most common in nurseries, seed catalogs: giant hybrids with flowers in white, blue, pink, rose, red, often with contrasting blotches; Wiesmoor hybrids with flowers fringed, crested, many colors. (See photo, page 92.)

S. saxorum. Very hairy, 1-inch leaves on trailing stems. White-throated, lavender flowers.

STRING OF BEADS. See Senecio rowleyanus.

STRING OF HEARTS. See Ceropegia woodii.

SUCCULENT. A succulent is any plant that stores water in juicy leaves, stems, or roots to withstand drought. Epiphytic orchids and cactus are commonly excluded from this group. Most succulents are native to desert or semi-desert areas in warmer parts of the world; Mexico and South Africa are two important sources. Some (such as sedums and sempervivums) come from colder climates, where they grow on dry rocky ledges. Most are easy to grow and require little care. Not all like hot sun; read species descriptions carefully. For succulents to grow indoors, see: *Adromischus, Agave, Aloe, Ceropegia woodii, Cotyledon, Crassula, Echeveria, Euphorbia, Gasteria, Haworthia, Kalanchoe, Lithops, Sansevieria, Sedum, Sempervivum.*

SWEDISH IVY. See Plectranthus.

SWORD FERN. See Nephrolepis.

SYNGONIUM podophyllum (*Nephthytis*). Arrowhead plant. Evergreen, slow-growing shrub related to *Philodendron.* Can be trained to climb, hang, grow upright with support. Has aerial roots. Easy to grow. Arrow-shaped, long stalked, dull green or variegated leaves. Likes standard potting mix, lots of water (can be rooted in water; will live there for unlimited period of time), average house temperatures and humidity, regular fertilizing. Can take most light situations: with lots of light, leaves bright green, large; in darker spots, leaves are darker, smaller, variegated leaves are more patterned. Prune to make bushy. Good in dish gardens, terrariums. Many varieties: 'Ruth Fraser', silvery leaves bordered green; 'Trileaf Wonder', green leaves covered with whitish powder; 'California Silver Wonder', narrow, silvery leaves. (See photos at right.)

TARO. See Colocasia esculenta.

TEMPLE BELLS. See Smithiantha.

THREADLEAF FALSE ARALIA. See Dizygotheca.

TI. See Cordyline terminalis.

TIGER ORCHID. See Odontoglossum grande.

Syngonium podophyllum

Syngonium podophyllum

Tolmiea menziesii

TILLANDSIA lindeniana (*Vriesia lindenii*). Epiphytic bromeliad with rosette form. Large flower spike has crimson bracts overlapping dense, flattened plume with small, bluish purple flowers. Plant in osmunda fiber, fir bark, or in a tree branch with a pocket of sphagnum moss. Likes bright light (no direct hot sun), average temperatures, good air circulation, regular fertilizing. Let potting mix dry out between waterings.

TOLMIEA menziesii. Piggy-back plant, Pick-a-back. Native to coastal mountain ranges from northern California northward to Alaska. Heart-shaped, apple green leaves with delicate fuzz and toothed edges. New plantlets grow on top of older leaves (at junction of leaf stalk and blade), giving nickname. Inconspicuous, reddish brown flowers. Likes filtered light, cool temperatures, standard potting mix, average indoor humidity, lots of water. Inspect frequently for pests. (See photo at left.)

TRADESCANTIA fluminensis. Wandering jew. Perennial vine from Central America. Grown for foliage. Frequent pruning needed to control size, keep compact. Fast growing. Succulent stems with swollen joint where 2½-inch-long, dark green, oval or oblong leaves attach. Tiny white flowers. 'Variegata' has leaves striped yellow or white. Likes standard potting mix, light from sun to shade, average house conditions, normal watering. Good for hanging baskets.

TREE FERN HAWAIIAN. See Cibotium.

TREVESIA. Snowflake tree. Evergreen shrub, small tree. Resembles *Fatsia japonica* in growth habit but taller (10-20) feet, more treelike. Leaves on long stalks, 1-2 feet across, deeply cut and lobed, resembling outline of enormous snowflake. Likes bright light (no direct hot sun from west or south exposure), standard potting mix with good drainage, liberal watering and fertilizing, average house conditions. Mealybug, spider mite may be a problem.

TURTLE ORCHID. See Oncidium ampliatum.

UMBRELLA PLANT. See Cyperus alternifolius.

UMBRELLA TREE. See Brassaia actinophylla.

VANDA. Epiphytic orchids native to the Philippines, Malaysia, the Himalayas; now grown commercially in the Hawaiian Islands. Plants grow erect with leaves arranged opposite each other. Open-faced flowers. Plant in osmunda fiber or ground fir bark. Stem needs support to anchor aerial roots. Likes warm temperatures (60° is maximum low), high humidity, good air circulation, lots of bright light, especially from November to February to set flower buds. Water lightly during winter. (See photo at left.)

    V. caerulea. Native to India. Large, 3-4-inch flowers from pale to dark blue on long stems; blooms late

Vanda

summer, early fall. Dark green, rigid leaves.

V. sanderiana. To 3 feet. Flat, 3-4-inch flowers in fall; combination of white, rose, greenish yellow, brown, dark red.

V. teres. Native to Burma. Flowers used in making leis in Hawaii. Flowers shades of rose with tinges of white, yellow; blooms from May to September. Needs winter rest, tremendous amounts of light.

VELVET PLANT. See Gynura aurantiaca.

VELVET PLANT, TRAILING. See Ruellia makoyana.

VENUS FLYTRAP. See Dionaea muscipula.

VRIESIA. Bromeliad with rosette growth. Feathery flower plumes. Some foliage mottled, banded brown. Likes bright light (no direct hot sun), good air circulation, average house temperatures and humidity. Keep "vase" filled with water. Let potting mix dry out slightly between waterings. (See photos at right.)

V. 'Mariae'. Light green leaves. Yellow flowers rise in clusters, are encased in bracts that are red at base, yellow dotted with brown at tip.

V. splendens 'Major'. Dark green leaves banded with deep, reddish purple underneath, lighter on top. Flowers yellowish white encased in red bracts.

WALKING IRIS. See Neomarica northiana.

WANDERING JEW. See Tradescantia fluminensis, Zebrina pendula.

WATERMELON PEPEROMIA. See Peperomia sandersii.

WAX BEGONIAS. See Begonia semperflorens.

WAX FLOWER. See Hoya.

WEEPING FIG. See Ficus benjamina.

WHITE FLAG. See Spathiphyllum.

YEW PINE. See Podocarpus macrophyllus.

ZEBRA BASKET VINE. See Aeschynanthus marmoratus.

ZEBRA PLANT. See Calathea zebrina.

ZEBRINA pendula. Wandering Jew. Evergreen trailing plant native to tropical Mexico and Central America. Same growth habit and leaf shape as *Tradescantia fluminensis* but not as hardy. Many variegated forms. Likes standard potting mix, some humidity, ample water. Variegated leaf forms need more light than all green ones.

Z. p. 'Quadricolor'. Purplish green leaves with longitudinal bands of white, pink, carmine red.

ZYGOCACTUS truncatus. Two plants have been sold under this name. For the best known of these— Christmas cactus—see *Schlumbergera bridgesii.* For the Crab cactus, see *Schlumbergera truncata.*

Vriesia 'Mariae'

Vriesia splendens 'Major'

Index

➤ **To find an individual plant description, look up the plant name, listed alphabetically in the Plant Selection Guide, pages 34-95. This index gives page numbers for general house plant information only.**

Photographers

Andrew R. Addkison: 75 top. **American Orchid Society:** 75 bottom. **William Aplin:** 18 right; 35 bottom; 41 top; 44 bottom; 73 bottom; 74; 89 center. **Dave Barnes:** 67 bottom; 71 bottom. **Glenn M. Christiansen:** 35 top; 92 top. **Robert Cox:** 76 bottom; 94 bottom. **Richard Dawson:** 42 top. **Gerald R. Fredrick:** 82 center. **Roy Krell:** 67 center. **Jack McDowell:** 43 bottom; 54 top. **Ells Marugg:** 7 top, center; 8 top left, right; 12; 13; 14; 25; 33 right; 36 center; 37 bottom; 38 top; 39 top; 40; 44 top; 45 top; 49; 50; 51; 53 bottom; 54 center; 55 top; 56 top; 58 center, bottom; 60 top; 61 bottom; 62 top; 63 bottom; 65; 66; 67 top; 69 bottom; 70; 71 top; 72 top; 73 top, center; 78 top; 79 top, center; 80; 81; 82 top, bottom; 83 bottom; 84; 85 top, center; 86 bottom; 87; 88; 89 top, bottom; 90 top; 91; 93 top. **Don Normark:** 4; 6; 7 bottom; 16; 20; 21; 23; 27 top left, right; 35 center; 36 bottom; 37 top; 38 bottom; 39 center; 42 bottom; 43 top; 45 bottom; 47 bottom; 48 top; 54 bottom; 55 center, bottom; 56 bottom; 59 bottom; 61 top; 64; 71 center; 79 bottom; 85 bottom. **Norman A. Plate:** 8 bottom left; 27 bottom; 32; 33 left; 34; 39 bottom; 52 top; 59 top; 60 bottom; 61 center; 63 top; 76 top. **Ken and Gerrie Reichard:** 68 top. **Jim Scolman:** 22 right; 41 bottom. **Betty Stoehr:** 68 bottom; 90 bottom; 92 bottom. **Darrow M. Watt:** 10; 11; 18 left; 19; 22 left; 30; 36 top; 46; 47 top; 52 bottom; 53 top; 57; 58 top; 62 bottom; 69 top; 72 bottom; 77; 78 bottom; 83 top; 86 top; 93 bottom; 95. **Peter Whiteley:** 48 bottom; 94 top.